THE VOICE OF HIS PRAISE

A New Appreciation of Hymnody

J. Edward Moyer

Henry M. Bullock, GENERAL EDITOR

GRADED PRESS • NASHVILLE, TENNESSEE

THE VOICE OF HIS PRAISE

Copyright © 1965 by Graded Press

All rights in this book are reserved.
No part of the book may be reproduced in any
manner whatsoever without written permission of
the publishers except brief quotations embodied in
critical articles or reviews. For information address
Graded Press, Nashville, Tennessee.

Scripture quotations unless otherwise noted are from
the Revised Standard Version of the Bible, copyrighted
1946 and 1952 by the Division of Christian Education,
National Council of Churches, and are used by permission.

ISBN 0-687-43948-5

SET UP, PRINTED, AND BOUND BY THE
PARTHENON PRESS AT NASHVILLE
TENNESSEE, UNITED STATES OF AMERICA.

FOREWORD

Surely the Christian hymn is the most widely used musical and literary form in our culture. Multiply the number of persons attending worship services and church schools each Sunday by the number of hymns sung and the total will be an astounding figure. Yet, while courses in literature and music appreciation are offered at the high school and college levels, serious study of our hymnody is practically nonexistent. The church should provide instruction to increase understanding and appreciation of hymns, and it is our fervent hope that this book may aid in discharging this responsibility.

To accomplish our purpose, we shall discuss the characteristics of good hymn texts and tunes and point to the presence of these qualities in specific hymns. This study should equip the reader with a set of standards so that he may respond with understanding and appreciation to good hymns and may learn to apply these standards to all hymns, familiar or unfamiliar.

As our study is based on the philosophy that appreciation without use is of little value, considerable attention is given to the "know-how" of hymnody. How should hymns be selected? How can they be introduced most effectively? How should they be interpreted? This is not an armchair study for the dilettante. It should be a practical encounter, with *explanation* and *experience* always in balance.

In many instances, because of space limitation, we can present only a brief excerpt from a hymn; but if the reader has the entire hymn available, other helpful observations can be made. Also, the diligent student will go beyond the specific hymns mentioned to find others that contain similar characteristics. This book attempts to suggest insights and to stimulate interest and curiosity; it is not a comprehensive treatise. Each area discussed is "open-ended." The reader is encouraged to continue the quest.

A word should be said about "hymn stories," if for no other reason than to explain their absence from this volume. Many books of hymn stories have been published, and the only information on hymns that many of us have consists of anecdotes regarding the composition of the hymn or a later experience in connection with its use. Such stories are interesting, but rarely do they help us understand the central message of the hymn. Therefore this book omits hymn stories in favor of a confrontation with the inner substance of the hymn itself, providing opportunity for a spiritually rewarding experience.

Although the history of hymns is closely related to hymn appreciation, a comprehensive history is not possible in this book. Chapter 10 provides an outline of the times, movements, persons, and a sampling of the hymns that furnish the dynamic of Protestant hymnody.

If this study helps the reader become more sensitive, more appreciative, more understanding, more enthusiastic in relation to the "Songs of Zion," so that he and those he guides will sing not only with their voices but also with their minds and hearts, our prayer will have been answered and our purpose realized.

—J. Edward Moyer

CONTENTS

1. *The Christian Hymn* 7
2. *The Hymn Text—Content and Language* 17
3. *Musical Quality and Fitness* 40
4. *The Hymn and the Individual* 54
5. *Selecting Hymns* 64
6. *Presenting Hymns* 72
7. *Interpretation of Hymns* 93
8. *Understanding and Using the Hymnal* not assigned 106
9. *Hymn Services* ...... not assigned 120
10. *Our Heritage of Hymns* 126
    Bibliography 159

CHAPTER 1

The Christian Hymn

JESUS, ON THE NIGHT BEFORE HIS CRUCIFIXION, SANG A HYMN together with his disciples as an act of religious celebration (Matthew 26:30). Paul quoted from early hymns in certain of his epistles and admonished his Ephesian and Colossian friends to sing "psalms and hymns and spiritual songs," making melody in their hearts to the Lord (Ephesians 5:18-19; Colossians 3:16). Martin Luther, recognizing that each person must comprehend his own faith and express his own devotion through meaningful acts of worship, labored untiringly to produce hymns that could be sung by the people in their own language. John and Charles Wesley, strongly influenced by the hymn singing of the Moravians, determined that singing should be an essential part of the early class meetings and went on to publish a steady stream of hymn collections for "the people called Methodists."

The high regard in which these men held hymns and the significant importance to which they attached the writing and singing of them is obvious to all students of hymnology. Indeed almost every great spiritual reawakening has expressed itself through hymns, using the texts to state the truth and spirit of the revelation and calling on the tunes to provide a lyrical means of supporting and transporting the messages in order to solicit the commitment of those who hear and sing them. Evangelical Protestantism believes that the sincere and thoughtful singing of great hymns can notably enrich the Christian life. Our premise is that this potential enrichment will be more widely realized if careful attention is given to specific aspects of hymn study.

The Christian Hymn Defined

On the theory that meaningful appreciation and experience must begin with understanding, let us first seek a definite explanation of the hymn as a form of religious expression.

We are obliged to recognize that the Protestant hymn has its roots in the Old Testament psalms and in the Greek and Latin hymns of the post-apostolic and medieval periods. But as we shall see, the fourth-century definition of a hymn as "praises to God with singing" is no longer satisfactory.[1] Surely in our day hymns have purposes other than praise; moreover, not all good hymns are addressed to God. The need for a contemporary definition is apparent.

Obviously many splendid definitions have been developed between the time of the church fathers and the present day. Rather than reproduce these, let us attempt to construct a definition that will encompass certain ideas to be advanced in this book:

A Christian hymn is a lyrical devotional poem set to an appropriate tune, in the singing of which an individual or group may offer praise and prayer to God, witness to Christian experience, and affirm Christian spiritual and ethical insights for the individual and society—all of these aimed at building Christlike persons for a Christlike community.

First, note the adjective *Christian*. Although hymns have been used in connection with many non-Christian or heathen

---

[1] While commonly attributed to Augustine, this definition is thought by some musicologists to have been written by Ambrose of Milan.

religious celebrations, we do not use the term in any but the Christian sense. For use in the Christian context, a hymn must be tested as to whether its content is in keeping with the message of the Judeo-Christian religion as revealed in the Old and New Testaments.

Second, the definition indicates that the text is basic and that the tune set to the text must help to communicate the spirit and message of the words. This does not imply that the tune is less important than the text, but it does suggest that tunes must be chosen with great care if they are to transport and enhance the texts as they should.

Next, let us note the terms *lyrical* and *devotional*. While hymns may serve a teaching function, they must accomplish this by use of devotional language. That is, hymns must be appropriate for worship, and Christian nurture will take place without sacrificing either the spirit of worship or the language of devotion.

Observe this principle applied in one of the newer hymns, S. Ralph Harlow's "O Young and Fearless Prophet." This hymn is certainly prophetic, calling attention to conditions in society that are not what they ought to be, and it suggests the application of Jesus' teachings to these problems. Although the text is virtually a sermon in song, the author does not threaten or scold but rather frames the hymn in the language of prayer and penitence. The hymn contains tremendous insights but presents them in the spirit of devotion:

O young and fearless Prophet, we need Thy presence here,
   Amid our pride and glory to see Thy face appear;
Once more to hear Thy challenge above our noisy day,
   Again to lead us forward along God's holy way.[2]

[2] From *The Methodist Hymnal.* Copyright renewal 1963 by S. Ralph Harlow. Used by permission of Abingdon Press.

If a hymn text is to be lyrical, the words must be well adapted to singing. Perhaps this requirement can be illustrated most dramatically with a negative example. Among the most unlyrical materials are certain of the early metrical psalms. We must remember that the aim of the metrical psalmist was usually to stay as close as possible to the language of the Bible; therefore we would not expect him to consider such matters as the lyric quality of his settings. In colorful language the author of the preface of the *Bay Psalm Book* justifies the literalistic approach when he maintains, "God's altar needs not our polishings." Such settings as the following may have satisfied the consciences of the literalists, but they certainly were not lyrical and therefore were neither widely nor enthusiastically sung:

> And said He would not them waste; had not
>   Moses stood (whom he chose)
> For him i'th breach; to twine his wrath
>   Lest that he should waste those.[3]

The words *appropriate tune* in our definition suggest the importance of unity—text and tune co-operating in a partnership in which each strengthens the other. In many of the great German hymns there is perfect mating of text and tune, and we would never consider using alternate tunes to hymns such as "A Mighty Fortress" or "Now Thank We All Our God." Nor would we alienate "Holy, Holy, Holy" from John B. Dykes' tune "Nicaea" or "The God of Abraham Praise" from the Hebrew melody "Leoni," so uniquely appropriate are these tunes for the texts with which they are mated.

Implicit in our definition is the principle that a hymn fulfills its purpose only as it is actually sung by an individual

---

[3] Taken from the *Bay Psalm Book*, the first book of praise produced in the American colonies, published in 1640 in New England.

or group. Appreciation apart from use is incomprehensible. Not only must hymns be sung, but certain purposes must be served in the singing of them. As our definition states, hymns are means of "praise and prayer"; they help us voice our petitions, our penitence, our aspirations, our consecration. Moreover, they contain affirmations and insights concerning God, Christ, man, and the Christian way, as revealed in the Bible and in human experience.

Our definition also expresses the conviction that hymns may challenge the attitudes and actions of society as well as those of the individual. Christlike living involves not only upreach to God but also outreach to our fellowmen. Piety without compassion is a travesty! To worship without feeling any responsibility for applying the ethics of Jesus in the community and in the world indicates only half a religion. For every hymn of praise, like "Holy, Holy, Holy," there should be a hymn of brotherhood, like "O Brother Man, Fold to Thy Heart Thy Brother." For every hymn of upreach, like "Breathe on Me, Breath of God," there should be a hymn of outreach, like "Where Cross the Crowded Ways of Life." The balance, marking the religious life of the mature Christian as he reaches up to God in prayer and praise and out to his fellows in loving concern, should also be present in the body of hymns that are used in the church and church school.

Finally, all these values and purposes reach their fulfillment when, in the sincere singing of great hymns, we are motivated and inspired to act on the truths we have been expressing until, as our definition puts it, we are led to become "Christlike persons for a Christlike community."

Characteristics of the Hymn Form

In order for a hymn to be sung by a group of people, it must possess certain characteristics. First, a hymn is metrical, with a controlled number of syllables in each line. To discover just what this means, examine Psalms 23 in the Bible and compare it with the metrical setting of this psalm below. The paraphraser has set for himself a metrical limitation so that there will be four-line stanzas, the lines having 8, 6, 8, and 6 syllables respectively. In the first stanza, the result is:

> The Lord's my shepherd, I'll not want;
>   He makes me down to lie
> In pastures green; He leadeth me
>   The quiet waters by.[4]

A verse-by-verse comparison of the Biblical and metrical settings points up the skill with which prose as found in the Bible has been rearranged to provide regularity of meter and rhyme. Why was this rearrangement necessary? Because, being unmetrical, the twenty-third psalm in its biblical form cannot be sung to a hymn tune; it can be sung only to a chant, in which the chanting tone provides for the irregular number of syllables in the various lines. Obviously then, whenever we use the psalms as hymns, they must be paraphrased in metrical form.

In addition to being metrical and rhymed, hymns are also strophic. A strophic song is more easily learned because the same tune is used for a series of stanzas. Strophic songs may be contrasted with through-composed songs in which the musical material is not repeated stanza by stanza but is developed according to the meaning and mood of the text. "Sunset and Evening Star," Tennyson's hymn to the music of Joseph Barnby, is one of the very few through-composed hymn tunes, and it is rarely sung by a congregation.

[4] Taken from the Scottish Psalter, 1650.

Then too, hymns are usually syllabic. That is, there is usually only one note to each syllable, a principle followed in some of our finest hymns. An example is the splendid "Lobe den Herren."

Praise to the Lord, the Al-might-y, the King of cre - a-tion!

In contrast notice that in the tune "Ariel" five of the eight syllables in the line are sung to more than one note each, making this an awkward setting.

Let all— on earth— their voic - es— raise,—

Another characteristic of a hymn that contributes to its "singability" is recurring accent. In addition to having a regular number of syllables per line, a metrical hymn is characterized by a recurring pattern of strong and weak pulses, of accent and relaxation. This quality permits a large group of worshipers to move together even without special musical training. Congregational participation in complex musical forms is impractical, but the hymn form with regularly recurring pulse and rhythmic patterns invites significant participation by all worshipers.

A final basic characteristic of hymns is the melodic nature of the tunes, together with the fact that the melodies are found in the upper or soprano part. A tune with attractive melodic interest is more easily memorized than a dull, uninteresting succession of tones. More will be said about qualities of hymn tunes in Chapter 3.

These are the characteristics of hymns that contribute

toward relative ease of performance and thus make possible hearty congregational singing.

Hymns and Gospel Songs Contrasted

In contrast to the hymn definition considered above, *a gospel song may be defined as a popular, highly rhythmic tune combined with a religious text of an intimate and emotional character in which the individual rather than God is generally the center of concern.*

The serious student of hymn appreciation will try to avoid taking a prejudiced position for or against that category of popular hymnody commonly referred to as gospel songs. Many persons dislike the label *gospel song* because its use seems to imply that the hymns of the church do not contain the gospel. Unfortunately no one has come up with a suitable substitute. Our approach will be to attempt a factual, objective examination of the characteristics of gospel songs:

1. They are frequently repetitive, especially when they contain refrains.

2. They are concerned primarily with conversion and life after death, rarely coming to grips with the realities of daily life or the need for Christian growth.

3. They frequently embrace radical theological positions quite at variance with the interpretations commonly accepted in the major Protestant communions.

4. They are usually man-centered rather than God-centered. Their overuse may lead to a self-centered religious experience.

5. Their melodies, harmonies, and rhythms are sometimes associated with secular music and draw attention to the music and away from the text.

As gospel song texts usually are written by persons who are neither theologians nor poets, and the tunes are composed by persons with limited musical training, it is inevitable that the quality of the words and music is generally inferior to that found in the great hymns. We must hasten to add, however, that there remains a valid place for the gospel song in the religious experience of some churches and individuals. Many bitter epithets have been hurled at gospel songs by well-meaning and sincere devotees of higher standards in hymnody, but we cannot recommend the sudden exclusion of these songs until we have inculcated in those who cherish them an understanding and appreciation of the finer hymns of our heritage. Furthermore, precious memories attach to gospel songs emotional ties that are difficult to break, even after the mediocrity of the songs is recognized. So in this area in which growth in understanding and appreciation takes us in one direction but memory and emotional ties pull us in another, it is essential that all who select and lead hymns and songs rise above personal prejudice and move forward toward higher standards, but always with love, tolerance, and patience. Those who hold to high standards of hymnody should respect the sincerity of those who do not yet understand and appreciate the best hymns, and should try to lead them in developing such appreciation. On the other hand, those who champion gospel songs should be willing to examine their product objectively and apply the standards that will be developed in these pages.

Bases for Hymn Evaluation

Perhaps we are now ready to set up standards for the evaluation of specific hymns. Of course, no particular instructor or book can force higher standards on a student or reader. By its very nature, appreciation requires that each person develop for himself a sensitivity to beauty and meaning. Here are some basic questions that will help the reader discover sources of quality in great hymns and of inferiority in those of less worth. There are four categories: (a) adequacy of content, (b) literary merit, (c) musical quality, and (d) fitness of tune to text. We will try to show that every great hymn reveals its worth by a high rating in all four areas. Both hymns and gospel songs will either vindicate their usefulness or exclude themselves from serious consideration on the basis of this evaluation.

Why We Evaluate

A cursory glance at the chapter headings in this book will indicate that our ultimate goal is not evaluation for its own sake. But our encounter with evaluation will prepare us to select, to interpret, and to use hymns more effectively in Christian experience. At the end of our dream we see and hear children, youth, and adults not only singing words and tunes but really comprehending and experiencing the truths contained in the hymns of our Christian heritage. When this happens, there will be a return to the hymn-singing vitality with which Luther and his followers affirmed the priesthood of all believers and, with which early Methodists sang the hymns of Charles Wesley that "contained all the truths of our religion."

CHAPTER 2

The Hymn Text—Content and Language

IF AFTER THE SINGING OF A HYMN IN A WORSHIP SERVICE, THE question were asked, "What was the message of that hymn?" many persons would be embarrassed to realize that they had not really comprehended its meaning. This is not a new problem. John Wesley admonished his preachers occasionally to interrupt hymn singing to inquire of the congregation, "Now do you know what you said last? . . . Did you sing it as to God, with the spirit and understanding also?"[1] Whether in Wesley's day or our own, a lack of thoughtful concentration during hymn singing symptomizes spiritual indolence that is frightening. What can be done about this? Obviously we must first recognize the tragedy of casual, thoughtless singing and acknowledge this as one reason for our inability to discriminate between commonplace and superior hymns.

Surely we owe to God our thoughtful attention to the content of materials used in worship and Christian nurture. Any lesser effort insults the God we worship and the Christ we would follow.

Turn to a favorite hymn and read the text slowly and thoughtfully as if preparing to be tested on it. You will prob-

[1] Minutes of conference, 1746.

ably instantly recognize insights that never before had been revealed. A valuable way to get at the message of a hymn is to read the words as if they were written in prose form rather than as poetry. Why do this? While meter and rhyme are indispensable in poetry, they at the same time militate against comprehending the thought; for it is easy to lose oneself in the rhythmic lilt of the meter and the pleasing nuance of the rhyme but fail to get a mental image of the ideas expressed. Washington Gladden's splendid prayer hymn, "O Master, Let Me Walk With Thee" provides material for our experiment. Read the hymn directly from the hymnal. Now read it in prose form as follows:

> O Master, let me walk with Thee in lowly paths of service free; tell me Thy secret; help me bear the strain of toil, the fret of care. Help me the slow of heart to move by some clear, winning word of love; teach me the wayward feet to stay, and guide them in the homeward way. Teach me Thy patience; still with Thee in closer, dearer company, in work that keeps faith sweet and strong, in trust that triumphs over wrong; in hope that sends a shining ray far down the future's broadening way; in peace that only Thou canst give, with Thee, O Master, let me live.

Do we not usually sing the first line of stanza three thus: "Teach me Thy patience still with Thee"? A close examination of the text will reveal that "still with Thee" looks forward to the words, "let me live." Such problems of awkwardness indigenous to the hymn form will be solved only as study of this kind is undertaken.

In addition to placing the words in their right relationship by arranging them in prose form, he who would capture the message of a hymn should test his comprehension by attempting to summarize or paraphrase the message. This act requires the kind of mental involvement that will make the hymn *live*. Again turning to the Gladden hymn, it might be summarized as follows:

> O Master, help me serve as Thou didst serve the lowliest of men. I would have Thy secret, by which Thou didst help the toilers, the careworn, the downfallen, the sinful to look up. I would seek Thy patience—living closer to Thee as I try to find Thy spirit in my work, in my trust, in my hope, and in my peace. With these fruits of Thy spirit, I shall indeed live with Thee.

Only as we come to comprehend hymn texts in terms that are meaningful to us, only as we make them a part of our own mental and emotional experience, will we be prepared to evaluate hymns as to their content.

Adequacy of Content

We must begin with a candid admission. It is impossible to secure complete agreement as to adequacy of content in hymns; it is not necessary to do so. Not only do various denominations have their distinctive doctrines and emphases, but even within a given denomination there are differences in belief and interpretation. A specific hymn may be suitable for one group and wholly unacceptable to another. In spite of this fact our hymnals are amazingly ecumenical. We sing regularly hymns written by Roman Catholics, Episcopalians, Methodists, Lutherans, Presbyterians, Baptists, Quakers, Congregationalists, and Unitarians!

There is at least one good reason for this broad ecumenicity in our hymnody. Extreme doctrinal concepts are not found in hymns that are used across denominational lines.

For example, Isaac Watts expressed the traditional Calvinist doctrine of man's total depravity when he wrote:

> Lord, I am vile, conceived in sin,
>   And born unholy and unclean;
> Sprung from the man whose guilty fall
>   Corrupts his race and taints us all.

Obviously this doctrine of the nature of man would not be acceptable to many Protestant groups and so the hymn is no longer used. But when all of Watts' unsuitable hymns have been expunged, there still remain some of the noblest and ecumenically most acceptable hymns of our heritage. These hymns are not controversial but they give expression to the great affirmations of Protestantism on which there is general agreement. No denomination could possibly object to the message of:

> O God, our help in ages past,
>   Our hope for years to come,
> Our shelter from the stormy blast,
>   And our eternal home!

The student of hymnology will discover that many great hymn writers wrote hymns embracing radical doctrinal concepts that have caused those particular hymns or certain stanzas of them to be dropped. Concepts that were meaningful in one generation may at a later time no longer be held; for theology is dynamic, and Christian scholars are ever seeking a better understanding of the truth that God is trying to reveal to his children.

Just as each new generation of theologians evaluates and reinterprets fundamental concepts of the Christian faith, so each new generation of persons who work with hymns, as authors or as teachers or as members of hymnal committees, must share in the continuous process of selection and evaluation. Our purpose now is to discover the factors involved in the evaluation of content.[2] The questions to be asked do not provide for the promotion of one particular theological viewpoint over another. Christians holding diverse opinions will find these questions a useful method of putting specific hymns to the test.

1. DOES THE HYMN SAY SOMETHING WORTHWHILE? There should be no quarrel with the validity of this requirement. Disagreement may occur, however, at the point of defining what is "worthwhile." Perhaps it is not necessary to remove entirely this disagreement. It is important that pastors and laymen become aware of this requirement and evaluate and select hymns accordingly. For examples of so-called hymns that say nothing worthwhile, we might turn to certain nondenominational songbooks published by commercial concerns. Many of the songs in these collections would not be approved by a denominational hymnal committee, for when tested for their intrinsic worth, they would not receive a passing grade.

Obviously church groups using these commercial songbooks in preference to their denominational hymnals do not come to grips with this matter of worthwhileness. As a child I reacted to a new public school songbook on the basis of its attractive tunes. It never occurred to me to give much attention to the texts of the songs. Perhaps this method of evaluation is used by some churches and church schools who feel they must sing from songbooks other than their denominational hymnals. How immature is such an approach!

---

[2] The author is indebted to S. Paul Schilling for first suggesting such tests for the content and language of hymns. Schilling's article, "The Faith We Sing," appeared in the February, 1953, issue of *motive* magazine.

Let us now apply the test to several hymns that are well known and widely used across evangelical Protestantism. The first is the refrain that has been attached to Phillip Doddridge's "O Happy Day." The memory still lingers of a seminary student body and faculty singing this hymn as a hymn of dedication after the sermon of the day. Five times (for there are five stanzas) we sang:

> Happy day, happy day,
> When Jesus washed my sins away:
> He taught me how to watch and pray,
> And live rejoicing every day;
> Happy day, happy day,
> When Jesus washed my sins away.

Doddridge never intended this childish refrain to accompany his noble hymn. In his original the word "happy" appears only twice. By singing the refrain after each stanza, there resulted twenty repetitions of this term. The wasted time and effort was frightening, especially when we might have been committing ourselves to genuine Christian service by singing, "Thy life is still a summons to serve humanity."

Among the hymns and songs that might be challenged as to the value of their content are those in which the chief emphasis is on a mystical relationship with Christ that seems to limit Christian experience to a kind of spiritual ecstasy. The Christian life simply isn't like that, and our authority for this claim is none other than the Master himself. The Christian dares not lose himself in introspection. He dares not spend his time meditating on "visions of rapture," nor can he afford to be "at rest" in "his Saviour." Christ's call was not theological; it was a call to service in the way that he served. Many so-called hymns tragically make Christ an idol to be worshiped rather than a Master to be followed!

2. Is the message of the hymn clear and understandable?

Hymns are a form of poetry, and poetry by its very nature can be quite subtle, abstract, and vague. Thus it is necessary to test each hymn to determine whether it is clear and understandable. For an example of excellence in this area, consider William Pierson Merrill's "Rise Up, O Men of God." There are no strange words, no odd expressions with vague meanings, no veiled figures of speech that create ambiguity of thought. The message is simple and direct: There is wrong in the world, which can be corrected only as "men of God" put aside "lesser things" in a united effort to "serve the King of kings." This involves working for universal brotherhood as we try to follow "where His feet have trod."

On the other hand, Percy Dearmer's Resurrection hymn, "Life is Good, for God Contrives It," has not found wide acceptance because the ideas are cast in abstruse language, requiring literary sophistication that the average hymn singer does not possess.

> Life is good, for God contrives it,
>   Deep on deep its wonder lies;
> Death is good, for man survives it,
>   Lives again in better guise:
> This they knew the night they hailed him,
> When He came through that which veiled him,
>   Alleluya, Alleluya!
>   Smiling, wonderful, and wise.[3]

What is meant by "Deep on deep its wonder lies"? Or again, exactly what is implied in the reference to the Holy Thursday experience, "When He came through that which veiled Him"? How are we to interpret the words "smiling,

---

[3] Words by Percy Dearmer, 1867-1936, from *Enlarged Songs of Praise*. Used by permission of Oxford University Press.

wonderful, and wise"? A hymn must function within the experience of the persons using it, and so the vocabulary, the symbols, and the figures of speech must be clear and meaningful to the majority of those who sing it.

3. ARE THE THEOLOGICAL AND RELIGIOUS IDEAS IN HARMONY WITH NEW TESTAMENT REVELATION AND SUBSEQUENT EXPERIENCE AND INSIGHT? Again, the hymns that will satisfy this standard will vary according to the doctrines accepted by and the emphases lifted up by the person evaluating them. To probe deeply specific doctrines in hymns is beyond the scope of this book. Worthy of consideration, however, is Schilling's suggestion that there are two sources of authority: (a) the New Testament and (b) subsequent experience and insight.

Hymn writers are faced with the same difficulty as are ministers when they preach exclusively by the proof text method.[4] Preaching a sermon and writing a hymn on a text taken out of context are equally dangerous. Hymns then, as sermons, must express ideas relative to the faith that are consistent with the overall spirit and message of the New Testament.

Believing that God continues to reveal himself to mankind through men of vital faith and strong intellect, we consider revelation subsequent to New Testament times also to be valid as we establish criteria against which to measure hymn content. Normally the finest hymns in terms of content will in each generation come from the pens of the spiritual and intellectual giants of that period. Consider Martin Luther, John and Charles Wesley, Isaac Watts, John Greenleaf Whittier, Alfred Tennyson; and more recently Calvin Weiss Laufer, William Pierson Merrill, and Harry Emerson Fos-

---

[4] A scriptural passage adduced as proof for a theological doctrine, belief, or principle.

dick. These men had an enlightened understanding of the central message of the Christian faith for their time. In addition, God gave them the ability to express their insights in beautiful lyric poetry so that through their hymns the gospel is revealed anew.

Let us examine several hymns in terms of this important standard. A splendid twentieth-century hymn expressive of an enlightened concept of God is Fosdick's "God of Grace and God of Glory." The opening line of the hymn offers a cule as to the author's concept. God is at the same time a God of glory, the almighty powerful Creator of the universe and everything in it, and a God of grace who is constantly calling his children to repent, accept his forgiveness, and achieve new life through him. The text implies that God limits his own power by his dependence on man. As long as man insists on disobeying, God cannot use him to overcome the "hosts of evil" who "scorn Thy Christ." So God needs man at his best in order to bring about his kingdom in the world, and in his grace and glory he will hear his children as they call on him for wisdom and courage to discover and do his will. The wisdom and courage that come from God, says the poet, will

> Save us from weak resignation
> to the evils we deplore

and will

> Gird our lives that they may be
> Armored with all Christlike graces.[5]

"God Moves in a Mysterious Way," by William Cowper, presents a somewhat different concept of God, picturing

[5] Used by permission of Harry Emerson Fosdick.

him as one who is inscrutable, mysterious, and who appears to be confounding his children with his unpredictable behavior. The hymn assumes that God's wrath is responsible for the "clouds ye so much dread," and he is a "frowning providence" who behind his exterior "hides a smiling face." When we realize that Cowper wrote this hymn after suffering severe depression that led him almost to take his own life, the generally melancholy tone of the words can be understood. The contrast between Cowper's and Fosdick's conceptions of God is clear.

For an exercise in comparative Christology (concepts of Christ) in our hymns, contrast Jay T. Stocking's "O Master Workman of the Race" with Lydia Baxter's "Take the Name of Jesus With You." Stocking presents a Christ who through the character of his life on earth challenges his followers to take up their tasks and in his name move forward in the doing of the "Father's work." "Take the Name of Jesus With You" seems to suggest a mystical Christology that sees the Master's name as a magic formula that will bring feelings of hope and happiness. Perhaps both are valid conceptions regarding Christ's place in human experience, but thoughtful and sensitive Christians will recognize that the "hope of earth and joy of heaven" promised by the poetess can eventuate only when enough sincere Christians say with Stocking:

> O Thou who dost the vision send
>   And givest each his task,
> And with the task sufficient strength:
>   Show us Thy will, we ask;
> Give us a conscience bold and good;
>   Give us a purpose true,
> That it may be our highest joy,
>   Our Father's work to do.

This then is the kind of criticism to which ideas in hymns must be exposed. Although we have confined discussion to a comparison of hymns representing differing conceptions of God and Christ, there are many other themes with which the same procedure may be followed: man, salvation, the kingdom of God, and many more. The student of hymns will find his own faith deepened and more firmly secured as he evaluates hymn content in this way.

4. DOES THE MESSAGE OF THE HYMN IMPLY CONCERN FOR ALL MEN? No one would deny that religious experience is deeply personal and that hymns may provide emotional motivation toward Christian commitment. No hymn, however, worthy of use in the church or church school will convey the impression that God favors one person or group over another, nor will the hymn contain expressions that will lead the singer to take pride in his spiritual experience. Unfortunately some songs widely used in certain segments of American church life are couched in these terms. Where the materials used in worship—sermons, prayers, and hymns—are exclusively personal, there seems to be too little concern for others and religious pride regularly results.

John Oxenham caught the true ecumenical spirit of Jesus' teachings in his hymn "In Christ There Is No East or West." There is no suggestion in this hymn that Jesus selects one for blessings and favors not granted to anyone else. Rather there is a prayerful concern that all mankind may know the salvation of God and be drawn into one family.

> In Christ there is no East or West,
>   In Him no South or North;
> But one great fellowship of love
>   Throughout the whole wide earth.

In Him shall true hearts everywhere
　　Their high communion find;
His service is the golden cord
　　Close binding all mankind.⁶

5. DOES THE HYMN RECOGNIZE THE CLAIMS OF BOTH TIME AND ETERNITY? The content of many hymns deals almost exclusively with conversion and life after death, while the important present in which we are growing in grace and in service to God and man is practically ignored. Often these songs refer to this life as a terrible ordeal from which we will be delivered "in the sweet by and by." Would it not seem that hymns that are preoccupied with a longing for "heaven and home" are really an insult to God, for does not our faith maintain that the kingdom of God can be realized here and now in the heart of each believer and in the "Beloved Community" of the church? To consider ourselves strangers upon a foreign strand will hardly motivate us to strong virile discipleship.

This is not to say that hymns should not deal with death and the life to come. It is preoccupation with this theme at the expense of the living present to which we object. We find the claims of this life and the next placed in proper perspective in many fine hymns.

Charles Wesley sees life here and the life to come in proper balance in the hymn, "Forth in Thy Name, O Lord, I Go":

> Forth in Thy name, O Lord, I go,
> 　　My daily labor to pursue,
> Thee, only Thee, resolved to know
> 　　In all I think, or speak, or do.
>
> . . . .

---

⁶ From *"Bees in Amber."* Used by permission of Miss Theo Oxenham.

> For Thee delightfully employ
> > Whate'er Thy bounteous grace hath given;
> And run my course with even joy,
> > And closely walk with Thee to heaven.

John Greenleaf Whittier gave us what is perhaps the finest hymn on the theme of eternal life. It speaks eloquently of the simple, yet radiant, faith of the Quaker poet:

> > I know not what the future hath
> > > Of marvel or surprise,
> > Assured alone that life and death
> > > God's mercy underlies.
>
> . . . .
>
> > I know not where His islands
> > > Lift their frounded palms in air;
> > I only know I cannot drift
> > > Beyond His love and care.

6. IS THE HYMN REALISTIC TO THE TWENTIETH-CENTURY CHRISTIAN? The newer translations of the Bible point out in dramatic fashion how over a period of several centuries words change their meanings and idiomatic expressions lose their powers of communication. We have come to see that the substitution of a newly translated word here and there is intended not to take us farther away from the original meaning of the passage but to recapture for us the intended idea. If the problem is so great that new versions of the Bible are occasionally needed, is it not possible that hymn texts too can become outmoded and archaic so that they do not speak meaningfully to our day? We think, for example, of some of the missionary hymns of an earlier generation. In the nineteenth century, Reginald Heber

wrote a hymn that for a century was the best-known and most widely used of all missionary hymns:

> From Greenland's icy mountains,
>   From India's coral strand;
> Where Afric's sunny fountains
>   Roll down their golden sand:
> From many an ancient river,
>   From many a palmy plain,
> They call us to deliver
>   Their land from error's chain.

This hymn, now being dropped from some denominational hymnals, assumed a kind of "spiritual colonialism" in which the Christian West was called by God to deliver "heathen" lands "from error's chain." Of course, Jesus commanded his disciples to go into all the world and preach the gospel to every nation. But now we realize that in too many instances, we equated Christianizing with "Westernizing." Present-day missionaries do not approve of the smug spiritual superiority of the Western World implied in these lines. In fact, our brethren in Asia and Africa might feel constrained to remind the Christian West that we are not entirely free from "error's chains" ourselves!

For another view on missions, let us study Henry H. Tweedy's

> Eternal God, whose power upholds
>   Both flower and flaming star,
> To whom there is no here nor there,
>   No time, no near nor far,
> No alien race, no foreign shore,
>   No child unsought, unknown:
> O send us forth, Thy prophets true,
>   To make all lands Thine own!

. . . .
>Help us to spread Thy gracious reign
> Till greed and hate shall cease
>And kindness dwell in human hearts,
> And all the earth find peace!

A comparison of these two hymns on the same subject by men of relatively equal intellectual stature bears out the conviction that God is continually bringing to men a new revelation of his truth. I venture to say that there was not a clergyman in nineteenth-century England who could have produced a hymn like "Eternal God." But the divine-human encounter continues, and we who work with hymns must keep abreast of it.

There are, of course, other areas of religious thought in which changes have come about that render some eighteenth- and nineteenth-century hymns meaningless. These hymns should be put to rest lest their use lead to confusion and misconceptions on the part of those who sing them.

Language Quality

Just as it is possible to clothe poor ideas in magnificent language, so it is possible to express valid ideas poorly. In an art form such as a hymn it is essential that adequate content be expressed through effective language so that each aspect is worthy of the other. Finding the best words to clothe an idea is the task of the poet if his hymn is to be useful. Once again let us explore this concern by posing a series of questions.

1. DO THE WORDS CONVEY MEANINGS CLEARLY? OR IS THERE AMBIGUITY AND VAGUENESS? Although much of the effectiveness of lyric poetry lies in the imagination with which the poet utilizes figures of speech to make his writing vivid and

colorful, there is always the danger of selecting expressions that are not understood by the reader. Ambiguity and vagueness result when hymns contain poorly chosen words and phrases. The absence of colorful language does not necessarily denote poor poetry. Sometimes too many colorful words weaken the hymn. We have already noted that "Life Is Good for God Contrives It" suffers from the overuse of figurative language, although the content of the hymn is excellent. A similar vagueness is found in Sidney Lanier's "Into the Woods My Master Went." The metaphoric language in which "the olives were not blind to Him" and "the little gray leaves were kind to Him," may please the literary connoisseur but it hardly speaks clearly or meaningfully to the worshiper.

Lest we deduce from these two examples that foggy language exists only in hymns written by highly skilled poets, we should observe that similar lack of clarity results when authors use words carelessly. "Beautiful Isle of Somewhere" is a case in point. The word "Somewhere" in this song is so vague that an equally effective song might be called "Beautiful Isle of Nowhere." "If Your Heart Keeps Right" is another song in which words are used vaguely. To refer to the heart as something that "keeps right" is not only unclear, it is also ungrammatical!

Henry van Dyke has given us a hymn whose language is colorful and imaginative but at the same time entirely clear. "Joyful, Joyful, We Adore Thee" was inspired by the final movement of Beethoven's *Ninth*, or *Choral Symphony*, and it is to the main melodic theme of this movement that van Dyke's hymn is sung. Schiller's "Hymn to Joy," which in turn supplied Beethoven with the inspiration for this symphony and the text for the choral portion, furnished van Dyke with the "joy" theme, but the hymn text is by no means a translation from the German. Van Dyke's hymn is an entirely original setting in which he ingeniously uses terms from nature as symbols of the ideas he sets forth. His approach is revealed in the first two stanzas in which he makes use of nature terms in two separate, yet related, ways. First, *flowers* are seen as symbols of human hearts, *clouds* symbolize sin and sadness, *dark* denotes doubt, and *light* by implication indicates love and joy. In stanza two all God's works are said to be voicing their praise: *heaven, earth, stars, angels, field, forest, vale, mountain, meadow, sea, bird,* and *fountain*—all these "call us to rejoice in Thee." The remaining two stanzas deal with God as the "Lord of Love." The natural world is now placed in the background as the implications of the Fatherhood of God to the brotherhood of man are faced. Magnificently does the poet climax his message in the couplet:

> Father love is reigning o'er us,
> Brother love binds man to man.[7]

Here is a tremendous message couched in matchless poetry!

2. Is THE LANGUAGE FRESH AND ORIGINAL? Trite, commonplace language is bad enough in extemporaneous speech, but it is much worse in a literary form such as a hymn that will be used over and over for years to come. To tolerate repeated usage demands of a hymn text the ultimate in freshness and originality.

When the tremendous scope of his compositions is considered, Charles Wesley may well be the most original of all hymn poets. Having written in excess of 6,500 hymns, he did not always retain a high level of vitality, as when he wrote, "He dandled me upon His knee" or "a poor, guilty worm I am." But after all the dross has been cleared away, he still wrote more superior texts than any other poet.

[7] From *The Poems of Henry van Dyke* (Charles Scribner's Sons, 1911).

As an example of Wesley's literary skill, let us analyze the hymn "O for a Heart to Praise My God." That the author had a tremendous vocabulary and was a master of literary style is clearly evidenced here. Wesley begins to exhibit his skill with the second stanza. He meditates on the kind of heart needed to praise God adequately. Note the terms with which he presents his case; such a heart must be *resigned, submissive, meek, humble, lowly, contrite, believing, true, clean, renewed in every thought, full of love, perfect, right, pure,* and *good.* Not only is his choice of words superior, but original, meaningful figures of speech are used. In stanza 4 Wesley finds the perfect phrase when, after listing the qualities of a heart fit to praise God, he prays for "a copy, Lord, of Thine!" Finally in stanza 5 he climaxes the hymn with a completely original metaphor:

> Write Thy new Name upon my heart,
> Thy new, best Name of Love.

3. Is THE IMAGERY AND SYMBOLISM IN GOOD TASTE? There is little point in writing poetry unless the poet goes beyond a mere recital of facts and insights. Poetry is marked by a plus quality such as we have already observed in Wesley's hymns and will observe in others to be encountered in this study.

As an example of an overused symbol, we need only recall the many hymns whose chief theme is "blood," a necessary symbol along with many others but surely not one that should be overemphasized until it becomes a substitute for the truth it is intended to symbolize. To treat life as a "mountain railroad" or to pray for "a cabin in glory-land" is surely in questionable taste. Perhaps the outstanding example of poor taste in language is "The Bells of Hell," said to have been sung in the nineteenth century:

> The bells of hell go ting-a-ling-a-ling,
> For you but not for me;
> The blessed angels sing-a-ling-a-ling
> Through all eternity.
> O death where is thy sting-a-ling-a-ling
> O grave thy victory?
> No sting-a-ling-a-ling, no ting-a-ling-a-ling,
> But sing-a-ling-a-ling for me! [8]

Let us not make the mistake of assuming that such words as *blood, mountain, bells,* and *hell* will never appear in a good hymn. For example, van Dyke writes majestically of "field and forest, vale and mountain." [9] The literal reference to mountain in this context is quite different from the symbolic *mountain railroad.* Or in the case of the word *hell,* we sing without revulsion Isaac Watts's strong hymn "The Lord Jehovah Reigns," in which the poet says:

> Through all His mighty works
> Amazing wisdom shines;
> Subdues the powers of hell,
> Confounds their dark designs;

How differently the word in question affects us here than in the tasteless "The Bells of Hell." Since hymns are poetic and poetic writing is vivid and colorful, the onus of responsibility is on hymn authors to discipline themselves lest their poetical devices lead to perversion rather than to great literature.

One of the strongest hymns of the church, which becomes even more inspiring when analyzed, is Robert Grant's "O Worship the King." Using Psalms 104 as the source of his

---

[8] Henry Wilder Foote, *Three Centuries of American Hymnody* (Cambridge: Harvard University Press, 1940), p. 269.
[9] From the hymn, "Joyful, Joyful We Adore Thee."

paraphrase, Grant refers to God through the use of descriptive synonyms. God is "our Shield and Defender, the Ancient of Days," and again, "our Maker, Defender, Redeemer, and Friend." The poet describes God's care as a quality that "breathes in the air," "shines in the light," "streams from the hills," "descends to the plain," and "sweetly distills [an unusually effective word] in the dew and the rain." One cannot study this beautiful hymn, frequently sung with so little animation and zest, without being moved to feelings of genuine thanksgiving to the Almighty Ruler of the universe who also supports the feeblest and frailest of his children.

4. ARE THE WORDS WELL-CHOSEN FOR SINGING? In general, hymns are more easily sung and more effectively interpreted if their texts contain few if any words of more than three syllables. Long words can create problems of awkwardness that are difficult to overcome. One of the longest words in Protestant hymnody is found in Charles Wesley's "O Thou Who Camest From Above," in the second stanza of which we sing:

> There let it for Thy glory burn
> With inextinguishable blaze,

On the other hand, the hymn "For the Beauty of the Earth" has a total of only four three-syllable words in the entire hymn. Hymn texts can have beauty and character without being overloaded with long, fancy words that may in the end keep the hymn from being singable.

Awkwardness may also be caused by successions of nonvocal consonants that are difficult to enunciate properly. Then, too, these successive noise elements cause too long a gap between vowels, thus preventing the smooth continuous line of tone that should prevail in singing. Benjamin Copeland's "Christ's Life Our Code, His Cross Our Creed" contains rich insights but suffers from an excess of consonants. If the reader will simply read aloud this opening line of the hymn, he will experience the awkwardness to which I refer. The alliteration of *Christ's, code, cross,* and *creed* is, of course, quite effective, but when the words are sung, the problem is very real. This is one of many fine sacred poems that are effective when read, less so when sung.

5. IS THE VOCABULARY VARIED OR REPETITIOUS? While repetition wisely used is an effective literary divice, where it results simply because a hymn happens to have a refrain or chorus, it can be a deadly and tiresome thing. We have already noted the repetition of "O Happy Day." A similar phenomenon occurs in "Saviour, Like a Shepherd Lead Us," in which the phrase "Blessed Jesus" is sung sixteen times. Another example is "I Love to Tell the Story," in which in the four stanzas these words are sung a total of fifteen times, with slight variations. In the four stanzas of "I Need Thee Every Hour" the phrase "I need thee" occurs sixteen times. Perhaps the epitome of repetition is found in this familiar refrain:

> For you I am praying, for you I am praying,
> For you I am praying, I'm praying for you.

In hymns of outstanding quality repetition will be used with discrimination, and frequently when ideas are repeated, fresh expressions or synonyms will be used. A classic example of this technique is Whittier's hymn "We May Not Climb the Heavenly Steeps," which illustrates the great poet's skill in this area:

> The healing of His seamless dress
>   Is by our beds of pain;
> We touch Him in life's throng and press,
>   And we are whole again.

Lines three and four repeat the central idea of the first two but with fresh language and strengthened impact. An even more striking example is the stanza:

> O Lord and Master of us all:
>   Whate'er our name or sign,
> We own Thy sway, we hear Thy call,
>   We test our lives by Thine!

We see here how skillfully Whittier builds his climax in the three concluding *we* phrases, each phrase moving up a step from the one before in a mounting crescendo of commitment!

Hymns Must Be Inspired and Inspiring

In this chapter we have introduced certain standards of content and literary quality that hymns must satisfy if they are to minister to a generation of literate and cultured persons. We have maintained that hymns should possess acceptable Christian insights, and that these insights should be expressed in beautiful, vivid language. This emphasis on worthy conceptual and literary standards does not mean that there is no place in hymn texts for feeling and inspiration. True, many hymns still in use consist solely of emotional expressions with little intellectual substance. These hymns are properly labeled sentimental. On the other hand, vital religious experience can never be confined to the realm of the intellectual. Good concepts, beautiful language, emotional vitality—all must be balanced if hymns are to feed both the minds and the spirits of those who sing them.

The Christian church looks longingly to a hymn-writing renaissance. Is it too much to expect that the remaining decades of the twentieth century may produce hymn authors who will write for this age as well as did Watts and Wesley for the century in which they lived? We await a great revival of hymn writing when inspired men and women will apply their literary skills to great spiritual truths in a mighty effort to provide new hymns for a new age!

CHAPTER 3

Musical Quality and Fitness

Quality of the Tune

IN EVALUATING HYMN TEXTS FOR ADEQUATE CONTENT AND literary merit, it was possible to be quite specific in setting down principles and finding illustrations. The evaluation of musical quality is more difficult, for it is not always clear why one musical setting is deemed superior while another is not. In fact, musicians of equal stature do not always agree on the quality of a given musical selection. Before proceeding with specific questions relative to tunes, we must realize that inherent musical excellence in a hymn tune may be cancelled out by faulty performance. One can perform great hymn tunes like "Ein' Feste Burg" or Ralph Vaughan Williams' "Sine Nomine" so poorly that their inherent quality does not come through. Or one can take a commonplace, trivial tune and lift it above itself by skillful, tasteful preformance. In this chapter, however, we will consider those qualities that must be written into hymn tunes if they are to transport texts effectively and make possible inspiring worship experiences for those who sing them.

We shall apply six challenging tests, illustrating each with appropriate examples.

1. Is the melody modest enough to keep the singer's attention on the text? The power of pure, pristine melody to create the atmosphere of worship is shown in the simple plain song of the medieval church. The absence of harmony, the relatively small range, and the natural speech rhythms prevent these tunes from diverting the attention of the singer away from the message of the words. Music leaders in Evangelical Protestant churches would grow in melodic discrimination by studying these old tunes.

For an example from Protestant usage, we turn to Isaac Watts' supreme hymn, "When I Survey the Wondrous Cross," and contrast the tunes "Eucharist" and "Hamburg" with regard to this test. The latter tune, arranged by Lowell Mason from a Gregorian melody, is the essence of simplicity. In Watts' hymn the singer cannot help being deeply moved as he reverently contemplates the love that led Jesus to the cross. In the presence of this ultimate sacrificial love, feelings of awe, humility, and adoration sweep over him. "Hamburg" supports rather than dissipates these feelings through its limited range and its use of conjunct or stepwise intervals. The range is limited to five tones of the scale and there is not a single melodic skip in the entire tune.

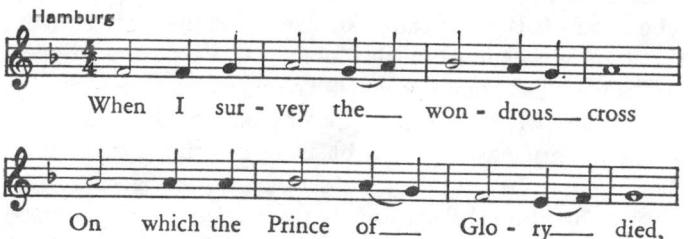

"Eucharist," on the other hand, is a busy, bouncy tune that seems to defeat the feelings of humility, awe, and adoration. Then, too, the false accent on what should be the unaccented syllable of "sor-*row*" in stanza three is unfortunate. That *row* occurs on the first beat or primary melodic accent is bad enough, but the problem is aggravated by the slurred notes which tend to place even more emphasis on the unaccented syllable. This is a perfect example of a hymn tune that violates our first principle of melodic simplicity.

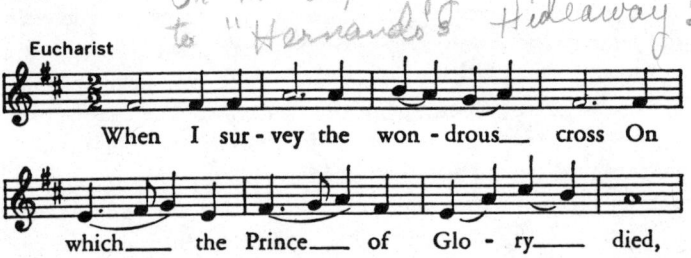

On the doxology to "Hernando's Hideaway!"

2. IS THE HARMONY APPROPRIATE TO THE MELODY AND TEXT?

Barbershop quartet singing is a perfect example of harmony becoming an end in itself. Indeed this phenomenon has made it possible for thousands of men (and there is a similar movement among women) with mediocre voices to produce thrilling effects. There is no objection to the pleasure it has brought both to those who sing and those who listen. It is significant, however, that the texts used in this type of singing are absolutely valueless from literary and conceptual points of view. The words are used simply as a means whereby the desired harmonic effects may be secured. This may result in pleasing entertainment, but it should never be mistaken for serious musical accomplishment or artistic achievement. Is the relevancy of this illustration to hymn tunes not apparent? Whenever the harmonies formed by the lower parts go beyond supporting the tune and draw the attention of the listener away from the text, we have harmonic idolatry!

In this connection it may be helpful to note certain harmonic progressions that characterize overharmonized composition. These progressions are not taken from particular songs but may be found repeatedly in music of the *barbershop* type.

There are purists among our church musicians who would go so far as to exclude all hymn tunes that make even occasional use of accidentals or chromatically altered chords (such as are shown above), even though these tunes are generally acceptable. While there is a certain amount of harmonic excess in the tunes "Serenity," "Rest," and "Hursley," these nevertheless have served great hymn texts well across the years. There can be ample opportunity for richness and variety in hymn-tune harmonizations without exceeding the bounds of good taste.[1]

3. IS THE RHYTHM DIGNIFIED AND IN KEEPING WITH THE RELIGIOUS CHARACTER OF THE TEXT? A person who enjoys music only when it has a "beat" is obviously still in his musical childhood. In music for dancing and marching, a firm beat is necessary because the primary purpose of the music is utilitarian, not artistic or spiritual. When religious songs

[1] For discussion of both sides of the argument, see Erik Routley, *The Church and Music* (London: Gerald Duckworth & Co., Ltd., 1950), Chapter 8, and Louis F. Benson, *The Hymnody of the Christian Church* (Richmond: John Knox Press, 1956), pp. 262 ff.

induce *foot-patting*, we can be sure that pulse has taken over and the text is no longer in command. Rhythm and pulse should not be confused. The pulse of a hymn should not be so obtrusive that it gets into the feet; rather it should be the servant of rhythm, lying beneath the music, as it were, firm and dependable but unobtrusive. Rhythm, properly understood, is the basis of movement in a hymn. Wisely used, it is determined not by physical sensation but by a proper understanding and interpretation of the text.

Certain rhythmic patterns by their inherent character call too much attention to the pulse and should be kept to a minimum. Surely the following rhythms quickly get the feet:

Let us not assume from this, however, that a hymn should be devoid of joyous rhythm. "Laudes Domini," to which we sing "When Morning Gilds the Skies," is a tune with rhythmic interest, though in no sense is there enslavement to a beat or pulse. The tune is transported by a spring-like beat, but the real rhythm lies in the way the melodic lines carry the text forward. Each phrase begins on an unimportant syllable with a light upbeat and proceeds to a climax on the final key word.

When morn-ing gilds the skies,— My heart a-wak-ing cries,

(Anthems are different!)

"Hark, how the bells, sweet silver bells";
"The Angel said to the women,"...

MUSICAL QUALITY AND FITNESS 45

That one rarely hears this hymn sung sluggishly is probably due to the fact that a good tempo is motivated by both the text and the tune. It is indeed a joyous tune but not without dignity.

4. IS THE TUNE SINGABLE IN TERMS OF RANGE, RHYTHMS, HARMONIES, AND INTERVALS? Only recently have hymn-book editors become aware of the importance of reasonable range in hymn tunes. Apparently it was formerly assumed that everyone in the congregation would sing a given part—soprano, alto, tenor, or bass—and the tunes were pitched with soprano voices in mind. Experience has shown that most people sing the melody, so it should be placed in the best key for the average person. The ideal range for the average voice is from *b*-flat below the staff to fourth-line *d*. While occasional *e*'s and *f*'s are tolerated, no tune should call for sustained tones on these high pitches. Among the tunes that suffer from excessive range is "Everyland, No. 1," set to Henry H. Tweedy's fine hymn "Eternal God, Whose Power Upholds Both Flower and Flaming Star." This tune ranges from middle *c* to fifth-line *f*, and in one instance the high *f* is held two beats on an accented syllable. Even when high tones are executed by a worshiping congregation, they are seldom produced with pleasing tone quality, for the required stretching of the vocal bands encourages muscular tension that prevents relaxed singing.

With regard to rhythm, harmony, and melodic intervals, we are concerned not with vocal problems but with those awkward difficulties that militate against accurate performance. The farther a tune departs from familiar scale and chordal patterns, the harder it will be to learn and remember. The tune "Wild Bells," to which Tennyson's famous New Year's poem, "Ring Out, Wild Bells," has been set in certain books, could well be the most unsingable tune ever admitted to a hymnal. One cannot imagine the average congregation successfully solving its melodic and rhythmic problems!

5. IS THE TUNE ATTRACTIVE AND EASILY REMEMBERED? Can a tune be free of the excesses discussed above and still be attractive? This question is posed because at times we are led to think that the alternative to an overly *pretty* tune is one that has nothing distinctive to say. Many useful texts are rarely sung because they are wedded to dull tunes. If a tune is worthy of being used in the worship of God, it should possess something of that beauty that God himself has made possible through his gift of music.

The recognition of the need for tunes that are attractive and that can be learned easily and remembered has led to the admission of folk hymn tunes to our hymnals. These

(Slane)

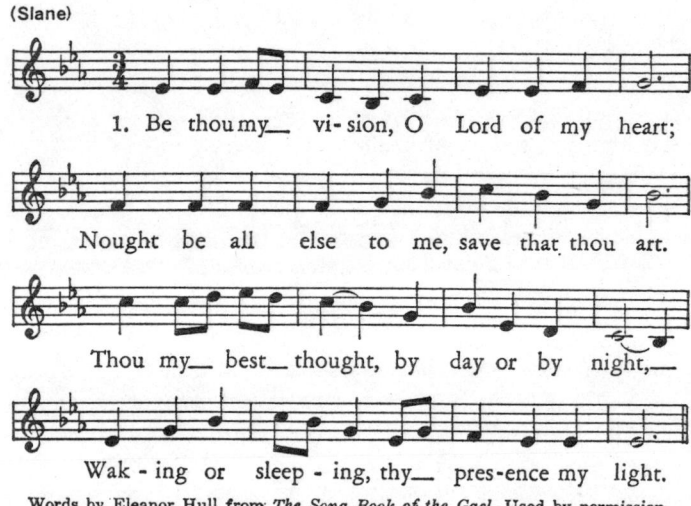

1. Be thou my vi-sion, O Lord of my heart;
Nought be all else to me, save that thou art.
Thou my best thought, by day or by night,
Wak-ing or sleep-ing, thy pres-ence my light.

Words by Eleanor Hull from *The Song Book of the Gael*. Used by permission of Chatto & Windus Ltd., publisher.

tunes are usually rich in melody and interesting in harmony and rhythm. Frequently they are intended to be sung in unison rather than in parts. The Irish tune, "Slane," set to "Be Thou My Vision," may be the most popular of these recently discovered tunes. Early American hymnody contributes its share of such tunes, one of the loveliest being "Pleading Saviour," to which "Jesus, Thou Divine Companion" is set.

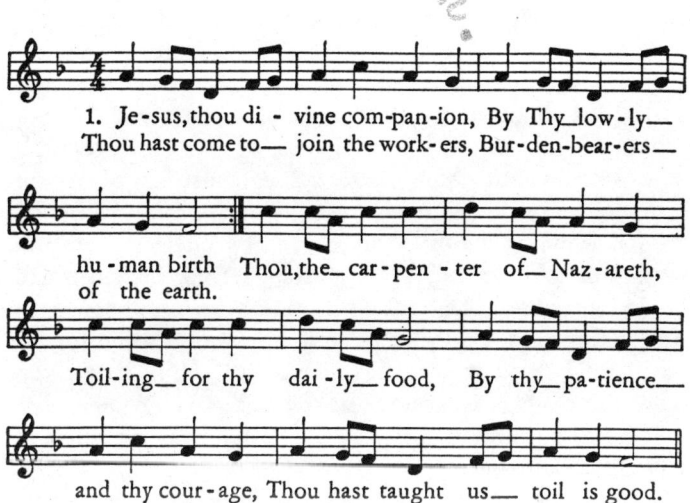

Words by Henry van Dyke. Used by permission of Harper & Row, Publisher.

6. Is THE TUNE CHURCHLY, OR IS IT MARKED BY SECULAR ASSOCIATIONS? We must become aware of two types of secular association that commonly make inroads on Christian hymnody. First, there are secular characteristics in melody, rhythm, and harmony. Joseph N. Ashton in his provocative book, *Music in Worship*, distinguished between *music in*

church and *church music,* pointing out that not all the music selected for use in the church satisfies the standards of genuine church music.[2] Some of these secular patterns have already been suggested. When we encounter songs possessing them, we cannot help being reminded of the type music in which they normally occur: musical comedy, waltzes, folk ballads, fox trots, or, in recent years, rock and roll. There are elements in the Protestant family that not only permit but recommend that our faith should be packaged in these secular musical containers. This tactic is justified on the assumption that thousands of unchurched do not respond to the gospel when it is communicated through traditional church music. The logic of this argument is not convincing. If there are eternal values to which the church must remain true, then these values must apply to the arts that serve the church as well as to the message of the gospel. Winning youth to the church by offering them the same musical fare they receive from the jukebox seems to be indefensible. The church is not a living room or a student center or a dance hall, and it must not "water down" its musical standards for the sake of attracting those who would not otherwise come. In the end, such compromise will be repugnant to the very persons it was intended to win.

Another type of association is that which surrounds specific tunes that originated in secular sources. Perhaps the best example of this type is "Londonderry Air," set in some hymnals to Tiplady's "Above the Hills of Time the Cross Is Gleaming." I first encountered this lovely Irish folk tune in the setting "Would God I Were a Tender Apple Blossom." Others learned it first as "Danny Boy." Can those of us who had a prior association with this tune ever outlive the earlier impressions? Some authorities feel that this is not a

[2] (Boston: The Pilgrim Press, 1943), pp. 28 ff.

problem, but the majority of sensitive churchmen prefer that our hymns avoid this kind of association.[3]

Another secular folk tune that has been given sacred words is "Home on the Range." The setting the author has in mind was obviously made to capitalize on the association, for where the words, "Home, home on the range," appear in the folk song, the sacred setting uses the text, "Home, home of the soul"! This is secular association in its most objectionable form.

In this connection someone may argue that the deeply spiritual "Passion Chorale," to which we sing the lenten text, "O Sacred Head, Now Wounded," was originally a German love song.[4] There are qualifying factors in this case: first, the association never existed among English-speaking congregations; moreover, much of the beauty and dignity were supplied by Johann Sebastian Bach's harmonization subsequent to its use as a love song.[5]

Fitness of Tune to Text

It may come as a surprise to some to learn that we are just beginning to work seriously at the matter of choosing tunes that will not only fit the texts in meter and accent but will also support them in mood and feeling. For centuries there were not sufficient tunes to go around, so it was necessary for certain tunes to be used with a number of texts. That this situation has existed well into the twentieth century is evidenced by the fact that in *The Methodist Hymnal* (1935) "Dundee (French)" and "St. Agnes" were set to five different texts each. There is now sufficient maturity in American church music and there are now enough well-trained

---

[3] For a defense of this hymn, see Charles Campbell Washburn, *Hymn Interpretations* (Nashville: Cokesbury Press, 1938), p. 34.
[4] "Passion Chorale" was originally "Mein G'Muth Ist Mir Verwirret," arranged in five parts in 1601 by Hassler.
[5] For Hassler's harmonization, see Erik Routley, *The Music of Christian Hymnody* (London: Independent Press, Ltd., 1957), p. 193.

church musicians so that no hymnal committee or editor need compromise on tune fitness. Every potential hymn tune should be evaluated as to whether it fits the mood and thereby strengthens the impact of the text.

Let us look at several aspects of text-tune fitness. Of course, there must be metrical agreement; that is, there must be enough notes to accommodate the syllables. But this is not enough, for there are many tunes in a given meter that would not fit given texts because the text and tune would not agree in mood and spirit. When a hymn is sung in a worship service or in a church school experience, its use should elicit feelings that will motivate the singer to make the ideas come to life in his own experience. It has been said that you can *teach* the meaning of goodness but you must *inspire* a person to be good. A good hymn is more than a teacher, it is an inspirer. It is in this process of inspiration that the nature of the tune becomes so important. It must give emotional thrust to the insights of the text. This can happen only when the tune agrees with and adds beauty to the message of the text.

It may be helpful to test this principle with a familiar hymn. When the tune "Campmeeting" was chosen for James Montgomery's hymn, "Prayer is the Soul's Sincere Desire," no attention was given to fitness. The combination was probably effected more by accident than by design. How does this tune support the text in mood and spirit? Not very well. The tune gets off on the wrong foot by placing a false accent on what should be an unaccented word: "Prayer *is* the soul's sin-*cere* desire." This accent on *is* occurs in five of the six stanzas of the hymn. Even more serious than this, however, is the fact that the tune is not appropriate in rhythm to the prayer spirit of the text. This type of rhythm, according to our experience, might be expected to accompany a folk ballad or a waltz, but it cannot possibly express the mood of Montgomery's text.

Let us look now at a more propitious combination of text and tune: the Welsh melody "Joanna" and the text "Immortal, Invisible, God Only Wise." The problem of such long words as *invisible* and *inaccessible* is solved by the way in which the tune moves in units of three-quarter notes to a beat. Though written in 6/4, the tune should be performed in "twos" rather than in "sixes," the time signature being interpreted as two dotted half notes to a measure. In this tune the melodic intervals seem to fit perfectly the mood of the words. *Immortal, invisible, inaccessible, almighty, victorious*—these words are majestic and thrilling, and the tune with its interesting leaps accentuates their majesty.

For a second example of excellence in text-tune fitness, we turn to one of the many fine hymns of German origin, "Ah, Holy Jesus, How Hast Thou Offended," as sung to "Herzliebster Jesu." The text of the first two stanzas offers a clue to the mood of the hymn and the type of tune that is needed to carry it.

> Ah, holy Jesus, how hast thou offended,
> That man to judge thee hath in hate pretended?
> By foes derided, by thine own rejected,
>   O most afflicted!
>
> Who was the guilty? Who brought this upon thee?
> Alas, my treason, Jesus, hath undone thee!
> 'Twas I, Lord Jesus, I it was denied thee;
>   I crucified thee.

This text is filled with remorse. We grieve not only over the crucifixion of the Son of God but over our betrayal through our individual sins and shortcomings. Surely if the tune is to be adequate, it must capture this poignant sadness and communicate the penitence that is expressed in the text. "Herzliebster Jesu" does this in several ways. First,

the minor tonality of the tune suggests a plaintive mood. Then too, the melodic direction of the tune is downward, and this is the appropriate inflection for sadness and sympathy. Finally, the metrical scheme 11, 11, 11, 5 is one in which the final syllables in each line are unaccented. In each of the words *offended, pretended, rejected, afflicted,* the accent must be on the second syllable and the final syllable must be very lightly treated. Both the melody and the rhythm of the musical phrase endings are conducive to correct accentuation.

Robert Grant's paraphrase of Psalms 104, "O Worship the King, All-Glorious Above," has already been mentioned in connection with fine use of imagery. When sung to "Lyons," we have another exceptional wedding of text and tune. In reading the text thoughtfully, one observes how in phrase after phrase there is movement onward and upward toward a climax near the end. For example, in reading the opening line, the interpreter will be led to accent the word *all-glorious,* while in the second line there is a steady ascent to the words *power and His love.* The tune with its rising melodic patterns always reaches musical climaxes on the strongest words. Surely it supports and strengthens the impact of the text.

FROM THIS ENCOUNTER with hymn-tune evaluation, both with regard to internal musical quality and fitness for specific texts, two objectives are sought. First, it is hoped that, by such exercises in analyzing as we have engaged in, the fine hymns of the church, which measure up so well when carefully examined, will be more deeply appreciated by our choirs and congregations. Second, this study should help us evaluate new hymns intelligently and select and use in our services those whose musical garments clothe the texts tastefully and effectually.

CHAPTER 4

The Hymn and the Individual

BECAUSE RELIGIOUS EXPERIENCE INCLUDES BOTH THOUGHT AND feeling, a person's response to hymns depends on both the appeal of the insights they contain and the emotions they engender. If the mind decides that a hymn is not worthy of being presented to God in worship, then the affection for the hymn based on its appeal to the emotions must be overcome.

The writer recalls a retired professional man in one of our great cities who would have been pleased to sing "The Church in the Wildwood" every Sunday. This song was associated with happy memories from his youth and childhood; and its appeal was entirely emotional, the thought content having little if any value. This example illustrates the way sentimental factors blind one to musical and textual standards. Our professional friend and thousands like him expect an intellectually honest and respectable sermon from their ministers. They object, however, when they are asked to sing unfamiliar hymns that will bestir them out of the lethargy into which the exclusive use of several dozen "old favorites" has lulled them.

Attitudes in the Use of Hymns

In an effort to probe more deeply into the psychology of the use of hymns, I suggest four attitudes, arranged in ascending order, which form a ladder of hymn appreciation.

Complete indifference	Desire to sing what is liked and what is familiar. Little thought given to message or musical worth. Sentimental response the objective.	Art for art's sake! Music and text viewed critically with emphasis on former. Little involvement and concern with message of hymn.	Area of sincerity. Hymns used as expression of worship and Christian experience. Personal preference and artistic values in background.

musicians

Those who stand on the first rung of this ladder will hardly be reading this book nor will they enroll in a course on hymn appreciation. It seems, however, that every Christian who regards God as a loving Father who creates, sustains, and redeems his children will consider grateful worship one of the prime requirements of life. If worship is one of life's basic requirements, it follows that the sincere worshiper will never respond to an act of worship—be it a prayer, scripture reading, or hymn—with indifference; but he will enter into the act by giving the closest attention to the materials being used. Kierkegaard's famous insight that God is the audience in worship and worshipers are the actors in the drama is a valuable reminder to those who are indifferent when a hymn is being sung. Even those who feel that they cannot sing have a responsibility to participate by reading the text and participating with their minds and spirits.

On the second attitude level we find the vast multitude of those who sing wholeheartedly only the hymns they know and like, resisting and resenting hymns that are new to them, no matter how excellent these hymns may be. This is the group that is most in need of our help; these persons must be reached if our efforts to increase the church's appreciation of hymns are to be fruitful. Can we lead them to see that God is worthy of the finest we can bring? Can we help them understand that whether a hymn is pretty or peppy may be important to the singer, but that God is not involved in this kind of response? If every layman and every minister, when selecting hymns, would remind himself of what worship is, his selection would be affected by this awareness, and we would then be taking a giant step to overcome the complacency and conformity that so severely limits our hymn singing.

The third rung of the ladder is occupied by those whose basis of enthusiasm for a hymn is determined by the text and the tune as artistic ends in themselves. This is a temptation that faces most professional musicians. A great tune according to musical standards and a great poem according to literary standards may combine to form a great hymn, but the hymn's greatness will not be spiritually effectual until we lose ourselves in its message. Musical and literary beauty are, of course, desirable, but these artistic considerations should not command our attention when we sing hymns in worship. Hymn singing in the church is unashamedly utilitarian. Its purpose is to bring the singer closer to God by stimulating his religious consciousness.

We have labeled the top rung of our ladder the area of sincerity. Indifference is out of the question. Personal preference on the basis of personal likes and dislikes ceases to operate. Artistic values now move into the background.

Hymns are regarded as exercises in devotion and as agents in the building of Christian personality. When congregations and related church groups approach hymn singing on this level, they will take an important step toward bringing new vitality into the life of the church.

What Hymns Do for Persons

Assuming that the study and use of hymns is approached with the attitude represented by the fourth rung of the ladder, hymns can then enrich the spiritual life of persons in several significant ways.

1. HYMNS PROVIDE A MEANS OF EXPRESSING OUR FEELINGS TOWARD GOD IN ACTS OF PRIVATE AND CORPORATE DEVOTION. Consider five progressive steps through which we normally move in worship and see how the opening couplets of carefully chosen hymns give expression to these attitudes:

Adoration—Holy, Holy, Holy! Lord God Almighty!
  Early in the morning our song shall rise to Thee.

Thanksgiving—Now thank we all our God
  With heart and hands and voices,
  Who wondrous things hath done,
  In whom His world rejoices.

Penitence—Dear Lord and Father of mankind,
  Forgive our feverish ways.

Aspiration—Breathe on me, Breath of God,
  Fill me with life anew.

Consecration—Take my life, and let it be
  Consecrated, Lord, to Thee.

2. HYMNS LIFT UP BIBLICAL INSIGHTS. All who teach and direct hymns should familiarize themselves with the scripture passages and/or ideas on which the hymns are based. Careful correlation guided by a thoughtful teacher will make both the hymn and its related scripture more meaningful. Certain denominational hymnals have handbooks in which a scriptural index is included.[1] Such an index is most helpful to ministers, choir directors, and church school music leaders.

Some hymns are paraphrases of psalms. They come to us out of the Calvinist tradition, in which hymns of "human composition" were not permitted on the theory that only what God has given in the Bible is worthy of use in worship. A comparison of the metrical and the original prose settings of such psalm paraphrases is an effective method of study. The oldest metrical psalm still sung is "All People That on Earth Do Dwell," a sixteenth-century English version of Psalms 100:

Biblical Version	*Metrical Setting*
Make a joyful noise to the LORD, all ye lands! Serve the LORD with gladness! Come into his presence with singing!	All people that on earth do dwell, Sing to the Lord with cheerful voice. Him serve with mirth, His praise forth tell; Come ye before Him and rejoice.

The same procedure may be used with other familiar psalm paraphrases: "The Lord's My Shepherd, I'll Not Want" (Psalms 23), "Through All the Changing Scenes of Life" (Psalms 34), "As Pants the Hart for Cooling Streams" (Psalms 32), "How Lovely Is Thy Dwelling Place" (Psalms 84).

[1] Robert Guy McCutchan, *Our Hymnody: A Manual of The Methodist Hymnal* (Nashville: Abingdon Press, 1937).

Other hymns are inspired by biblical incidents or insights and should be learned in connection with the biblical source material. For example, Charles Wesley's "Come, O Thou Traveler Unknown," considered by Isaac Watts to be Wesley's finest hymn, is obviously based on the incident of Jacob wrestling with the angel (Genesis 32:34).

> Come, O Thou Traveler unknown,
>   Whom still I hold, but cannot see;
> My company before is gone,
>   And I am left alone with Thee:
> With Thee all night I mean to stay,
>   And wrestle till the break of day.

In the broadest sense, every good hymn will be supported by scripture, and the wise teacher will take advantage of every opportunity to relate hymns to their scriptural roots whenever these exist.

3. HYMNS TRANSMIT THE CHRISTIAN HERITAGE FROM ONE GENERATION TO THE NEXT. Each epoch in the history of the church has made its own unique contribution in thought, in art forms, in religious customs. Sermons preached in former days are rarely read by any but professional scholars. Hymns, however, from many periods of history still are sung, and in the singing of them we catch a glimpse of the religious thought and language of the period they represent. And the message of many is timeless!

The American author who perhaps more than any other expressed his particular spiritual heritage through his hymns was John Greenleaf Whittier. As a Quaker, Whittier was not accustomed to singing hymns in worship. In fact, he wrote on one occasion: "I am really not a hymn-writer, for the good reason that I know nothing of music. . . . A good hymn is the best use to which poetry can be devoted, but I do not claim that I have succeeded in composing one." [2] Posterity disagrees with his self-appraisal. Foote places him at the top among American hymn writers: "Indeed, if widespread and continued use of an author's hymns be the test, he doubtless would be ranked, both in this country and in England, as the foremost American hymnist of the nineteenth century." [3]

Consider Whittier's hymn, "O Brother Man, Fold to Thy Heart Thy Brother." Its message is almost shocking in its implications. Says Whittier, all your beautiful chancels and magnificant organs and highly trained choirs are less than worship unless they are accompanied by a loving heart and kindly deeds:

> To worship rightly is to love each other,
> Each smile a hymn, each kindly deed a prayer.

And again,

> The holier worship which He [Christ] deigns to bless
> Restores the lost, and binds the spirit broken,
> And feeds the widow and the fatherless.

If we actually live after the example of Christ, we will enlarge our definition of worship:

> So shall the wide earth seem our Father's temple,
> Each loving life a psalm of gratitude.

This splendid hymn of brotherhood reveals perfectly that portion of the Christian heritage represented by this man,

---

[2] John J. Julian, *A Dictionary of Hymnology* (2nd rev. ed.; 2 vols.; New York: Dover Publications, Inc., 1907), p. 1278.
[3] *Op. cit.*, pp. 261-62.

his religious group, and his generation. It is our high privilege to accept Whittier's beliefs as our own through sincere singing of this hymn.

4. HYMNS INFLUENCE OUR ATTITUDES AND ACTIONS. Every sincere act of hymn singing will react on the singer, providing, through the insights of the hymn, motivation to lift the quality of his own life. Well-chosen hymns seriously treated in worship become a means of developing right attitudes in individuals and groups and of encouraging right actions, not only through the messages in the hymns, but because the sincere singing of them encourages commitment to live in accord with their insights.

A classic example is John Wesley's climactic experience on board ship bound for America when he heard the Moravians singing hymns of faith during a storm, at a time when he, an Anglican priest, was gripped with fear. Is it not probable that this experience was at least partly responsible for the important place the Wesleys accorded hymn singing in early Methodist meetings? So important were the hymns that it was said in eighteenth-century England that "to sing hymns was to be a Methodist!"

That moving experiences with great hymns still occur is borne out by a more recent incident related by Lina Rauschenberg. A college student was examining a drop of water under the microscope and was moved to begin singing

> This is my Father's world,
> And to my listening ears,
> All nature sings, and 'round me rings
> The music of the spheres.

Gradually other students in the laboratory class joined in a spontaneous chorus, affirming the greatness of God:

This is my Father's world:
I rest me in the thought
Of rocks and trees, of skies and seas;
His hands the wonders wrought.

A miracle of nature seen through the microscope recalled for this student a hymn that early in his life had impressed its message upon him. A laboratory discovery confirmed what he already knew: "God is the Ruler yet." How fortunate that the hymn resided in his subconscious, ready to be recalled at this moment.

Attitudes of little children, as well as of youth and adults, can be moulded by the singing of hymns that are meaningful to them. Madeline Ingram tells of the little girl, who on a weekday led her grandfather to the door of her church sanctuary, then turned to him and said: "In here we must whisper, for this is the house of God." This little one, through a song learned in church school or children's choir, had already developed an attitude of reverence that was expressed through appropriate conduct.

It is wonderful to contemplate the potential change in attitude and action if all of us who are privileged to introduce hymns to our growing children took full advantage of every opportunity to plant seed such as had been planted in the instances cited above.

5. Hymns contribute to cultural growth. The person who engages in hymn study cannot help but grow in his appreciation of literature and music. What he has learned in the study of hymns can have a bearing on his response to nonhymnic literature and music. For example, the hymn "Joyful, Joyful, We Adore Thee" may open a door to Beethoven's *Ninth Symphony,* and Bach's "Passion Chorale" may stimulate an interest in the many moving chorale pre-

ludes and cantatas of the German master. Sibelius' "Finlandia" may take on added interest after meeting the horn theme in "Be Still, My Soul." "The Spacious Firmament on High" introduces two great masters: Joseph Addison, who in the text exhibits the skill that made him one of the literary giants of eighteenth-century England; and Franz Joseph Haydn, from whose oratorio *The Creation* this hymn tune is taken. Christian culture and art are gifts from a generous God, and the learning and singing of hymns will lead to wider appreciation of these gifts.

6. SINGING HYMNS PROMOTES THE FELLOWSHIP OF BELIEVERS IN ACTS OF WORSHIP. In addition to the personal nature of hymn singing, there is also a sense in which when we sing we are part of a *Koinonia*, a fellowship of believers. We feel more securely involved in the family of God as we join with others of his children in this activity.

Inevitably the hymns that are most pleasing to God because they are the best we can offer in acts of worship are the hymns that will do most for us as persons. Where hymn singing operates on the lower rungs of our ladder, marked by indifference or limited by enslavement to familarity and favoritism, the values suggested above will not be realized. But when hymns that are worthy to be placed on the altar of our worship are sung with seriousness of purpose, the rewards in terms of spiritual enrichment will be unlimited.

CHAPTER 5

Selecting Hymns

MINISTERS AND LAYMEN ALIKE HAVE OPPORTUNITIES TO SELECT hymns for various types of services. Most of us who choose hymns give less time and thought to this task than we should. Consequently we overwork certain favorites and overlook many excellent hymns that should be discovered and used. Anyone who has a responsibility for choosing hymns should increase his own repertory to the point where specific hymns willl leap into his mind as he works at the task. But he should also keep in mind certain guiding principles. To these we now turn.

Liturgical Selection

Behind wise hymn selection lies an awareness of what the hymn is expected to accomplish in relation to the rest of the service. The steps through which we move in public worship are classified in various ways. We have chosen four basic acts: (*a*) *adoration*, worship given to God alone; (*b*) *humiliation*, the humbling of self to admit, and seek forgiveness for, our sins and shortcomings; (*c*) *redemption*, God's love revealed; and (*d*) *dedication*, personal surrender to God's love.

The first hymn in a service should always be related to the act of adoration. It is therefore a hymn of praise—

objective and God centered. Exultation, thanksgiving, reverence, and joy are among the moods consonant with this act. Many hymns are appropriate for the opening of worship. These are a few:

"Holy, Holy, Holy"
"Come, Thou Almighty King"
"Praise to the Lord, the Almighty"
"For the Beauty of the Earth"
"O Worship the King"
"Joyful, Joyful, We Adore Thee"
"Sing Praise to God Who Reigns Above"
"Immortal, Invisible, God Only Wise"
"Come, Sound His Praise Abroad"
"I'll Praise My Maker While I've Breath"
"Men and Children Everywhere"
"I Sing the Almighty Power of God"

The second hymn should normally relate to the second or third steps: humiliation or redemption. When the hymn is a part of the period during which the worshipers are looking inward and baring their hearts before God, it should be a hymn of penitence. The following hymns are appropriate:

"Dear Lord and Father of Mankind"
"Spirit of God, Descend Upon My Heart"
"If Thou But Suffer God to Guide Thee"
"O Gracious Father of Mankind"

Frequently the second hymn is placed immediately before the sermon or meditation, in which case it may be a general hymn of preparation, such as:

"Break Thou the Bread of Life"
"Master, Speak, Thy Servant Heareth"
"Talk With Us, Lord, Thyself Reveal"
"Blessed Jesus, at Thy Word"

The second hymn may also introduce the theme of the message, though it should not provide answers to the problems to be considered. It should introduce the theme but not "preach"; it should stimulate interest and involvement in the subject, but it should not anticipate the sermon itself. To sing such didactic hymns as "O Young and Fearless Prophet," "God of Grace and God of Glory," or "Where Cross the Crowded Ways of Life" before the sermon is to render the sermon anticlimactic, virtually unnecessary. These are great hymns, but they should be sung *following* the messages to which they relate.

Middle hymns may also be affirmations of religious conviction. Just as we affirm our faith through one of the historic or contemporary creeds, so we may affirm our convictions through a hymn. "There's a Wideness in God's Mercy" and "We May Not Climb the Heavenly Steeps" express truths that may be dealt with in sermons on God's providence and Christ's compassion respectively.

The final hymn in a service of worship should confirm the content of the message, challenge the worshiper to action, and motivate him to dedicate himself to the quality of discipleship conveyed in the message. Several useful final hymns are:

"Rise Up, O Men of God"—a clarion call to Christian action

"At Length There Dawns the Glorious Day"—a call to brotherhood

"O Jesus, I Have Promised"—consecration to personal discipleship

"Eternal God, Whose Power Upholds"—a commission to take Christ to all mankind.

Fosdick's "God of Grace and God of Glory" is a most effective final hymn. Its prayer for a fuller measure of the Christlike graces is broad enough that it can be used properly after a wide variety of sermons or meditations.

Thematic Selection

An obvious basis for hymn selection may be the theme of the message. In this connection we must distinguish carefully between the theme and the title. It is not enough simply to select several hymns that have words in common with a sermon title. Words like *love* and *peace* recur frequently in titles, but they are interpreted in many different ways. Intelligent hymn selection requires a knowledge of the gist of the message so that hymns will be selected that support the ideas presented. If a sermon on love develops the need for compassionate concern for one's neighbor, it would be unwise to choose for the final hymn, "O Love that Wilt Not Let Me Go," which speaks of the love of Christ as making possible a mystical relationship between God and man. Similarly, a sermon on world peace would not be supported by "Peace, Perfect Peace." Rather, it calls for a hymn such as "Turn Back, O Man, Forswear Thy Foolish Ways."

When hymns are chosen on a thematic basis, care must be taken that all the hymns do not say the same thing. That is, each hymn should complement, or add new insights, rather than repeat with variations the ideas in the other hymns. This kind of repetition sometimes results when we fail to read the texts carefully before making our final selection.

Ofttimes the theme of a sermon or meditation is too limited to permit selecting hymns that correlate with it. When this is the case, a distinction can be made between the *message* theme and the *worship* theme. The latter will be an umbrella under which the specific message subject naturally falls. A sermon might deal with personal morality, under the broader worship theme "The Kingdom of God," for God depends on the obedience of his children to bring his kingdom into existence among men.

well enough; you don't know your hymns or your sermon is trivial!

Liturgical-Thematic Selection

The ideal way to select hymns is to combine the liturgical and thematic approaches. The first hymn can combine praise with ideas relevant to the message. That is, from the large body of opening hymns, that hymn should be chosen which relates most closely to the sermon or meditation. The second hymn can also be chosen in this way. The third hymn is always thematic, because the dedication or challenge it brings is determined by the message itself.

As an example of this procedure, let us assume that on the Sunday after Easter the sermon is entitled "The Divine Victory," and it sets forth the proposition that the love that led Christ to the cross prevailed over sin and death and is an active force, drawing all men to him who loved. The sermon purports to show that in every person resides the potential of responding to this love by commitment to Christ and to the way of life he gave. If we select the hymns on the basis of the response we shall try to secure from the congregation, considering both the liturgical steps and the theme, we may decide on the following:

Hymn of Praise—"Ye Servants of God, Your Master Proclaim"

Hymn of Preparation—"O Master, Let Me Walk With Thee"

Hymn of Dedication—"Where Cross the Crowded Ways of Life"

Obviously, if this method is followed, hymns cannot be selected at the last minute or "on the run." An hour spent on this task may be a wise investment in time and effort.

Appropriateness to Age Groups Represented

Selecting hymns for a service attended only by adults will be far easier than for services in which children and youth are also present. At least one hymn in every service should communicate meaningfully to persons in every age group. Tennyson's "Strong Son of God" is a profound hymn dealing with the meaning of the Incarnation; however, it is intellectually over the heads of many youth and adults and completely unsuitable for children. In its place the simple though lovely "Fairest Lord Jesus" may be sung.

This does not mean that the primary or junior child should be exposed only to hymns that he understands fully the first time he sings them. To the contrary, children should be given the opportunity to sing hymns, the fuller understanding of which they will grow into as they mature. To introduce great hymns to children at a highly impressionable age is a privilege that must not be accepted lightly.

In contrast to "Strong Son of God," Heber's "Holy, Holy, Holy" is a hymn that draws an immediate response from children. In spite of "cherubim" and "seraphim," and other symbolism that is beyond their understanding, the hymn has a ceremonial quality that inspires children. Even the girl who misunderstood the final phrase of the opening stanza to be "God in three persons, blessed trim-the-tree" was not ultimately harmed by this childish misconception.

Fortunately many outstanding hymns are comprehensible to children and at the same time are suitable for adults. In small church schools where persons of all ages worship together, hymns of this type will be most valuable:

"This Is My Father's World"
"Fairest Lord Jesus"
"For the Beauty of the Earth"
"When Morning Gilds the Skies"
"Joyful, Joyful, We Adore Thee"
"Rejoice, Ye Pure in Heart"
"All Beautiful the March of Days"
"The Lord's My Shepherd, I'll Not Want"

Familiarity and Singability

In our efforts to enlarge the repertory of hymns used in our churches, it is possible for us to introduce too many unfamiliar hymns within a short period of time. The result of this poor strategy is strenuous objection on the part of the people to anything new. Perhaps a good rule is that one hymn in each hymn-singing experience should be well known, and no more than one should be unfamiliar. A new hymn should never be used as the opening hymn of a service. The opening hymn must be well known if the service is to get off to a good start. It is wise to obey this psychological principle even if this means that a new hymn of praise on the occasion of its first singing will be placed in the position of the second or third hymn of the service.

Musical and Poetical Variety

Hymn singing will be more rewarding if the hymns chosen for a given occasion are varied in rhyme scheme, length, tempo, rhythm, and mood. Three long, stately, slow-moving hymns may cause the singing to lose its drive and movement. Or again, three hymns with the same time signature may result in monotony.

Variety may also be secured by choosing hymns from different historical periods. If the opening hymn comes from the early metrical psalm period, as in the case of "All People That on Earth Do Dwell," select a middle hymn from an eighteenth-century poet, such as Charles Wesley, and a hymn of dedication from a contemporary writer such as Fosdick or Merrill.

1. HOW MANY DIFFERENT HYMNS SHOULD A CONGREGATION SING IN THE COURSE OF A YEAR? It would seem that 125 would be a fair minimal expectation, with no single hymn used more than five times during that period. Persons who have

the responsibility for selecting hymns should keep a careful record of the occasions on which the hymns are sung. The dates may be entered in the hymnal itself. Or it may be helpful to construct a chart in such a way that one can see at a glance what hymns have been sung and how often and what good hymns have been overlooked. Using such a chart over a period of a year will reveal overuse of certain favorites and other unwise practices in hymn selection.

Choosing hymns with careful diligence can be an exciting and rewarding venture. When well done it will bring the satisfaction of helping make possible memorable and meaningful worship experiences. Moreover, it will assure the use of a more representative sampling of the great hymns of the Christian faith, a desirable and commendable objective for every church.

2. IS A CONGREGATION OR CHURCH GROUP JUSTIFIED IN USING A HYMN OR GOSPEL SONG COLLECTION OTHER THAN THEIR DENOMINATIONAL HYMNAL? This is cause for serious consideration. The books to which they turn are not based on standards such as we are considering in this study but are produced for commercial interests. A denominational hymnal committee usually consists of ministers and musicians who work faithfully and diligently without monetary reward over a period of years to produce the finest hymnal possible. A congregation or church should not ignore hymnals so produced. This is not to claim that every hymn in a denominational book will speak with equal clarity to each member of the group. No congregation, however, within a denomination can find ultimate justification for turning aside from the carefully and prayerfully compiled hymnal of its group.

CHAPTER 6

Presenting Hymns

OBVIOUSLY WE ARE *presenting* HYMNS WHEN WE FIRST introduce them to a choir, church school class, or congregation; however, the process of teaching a hymn involves a great deal more than can be accomplished when it is first introduced. A great hymn rarely reveals its full beauty and meaning at the first hearing, for it needs to be studied far beyond the notes and the rhythms and the harmonies of the tune. Presenting hymns means helping persons discover the hidden beauties and deeper meanings they contain.

Those responsible for guiding adventures with hymns must equip themselves for the task. The observations regarding specific hymns scattered throughout this book can be used when these hymns are presented. The serious student will also learn to observe in hymns not mentioned herein the characteristics described below.

Where Can Hymns Be Presented?

It would hardly seem necessary to list times in the life of a congregation when periods of vital hymn singing and study might be scheduled. One instantly thinks of church school sessions, youth meetings, meetings of the men's and women's groups, choir rehearsals, fellowship dinners, and so on. These opportunities will be limited only by the imagination of those who plan these meetings and the availability of competent leaders. In fact, this writer believes that a meaningful experience in hymn study can be incorporated into a formal worship service without loss of dignity. In this setting the directions and insights must be carefully prepared. This is not the place for an informal approach. The success of a period of hymn interpretation in a formal service depends, of course, on the skill and method of the person in charge. Lovelace and Rice suggest that the period before the service of worship may be used.[1] Many of us will recall the fifteen-minute hymn sings that used to precede (and still do in some churches) the formal service. This pattern can still be useful, except that in place of singing simply for spiritual recreation, the session would be carefully planned with a teaching function in mind. In the long run, perhaps the children's church-centered musical and worship experiences offer the most attractive opportunity for building a singing church. Christian educators are now prepared to tell us the age at which specific hymns should be taught. If their suggestions are followed, the youth and adults of tomorrow will know more of the great hymns than is now the case.

The Psychology of Presenting Hymns

Many of us cannot conscientiously and sincerely lead groups in songs of little worth. At times we set back our efforts to improve hymn standards by the way in which we criticize the songs to which some persons are emotionally attached. In order to attain our ultimate goal, it is sometimes necessary to give more attention to preparing the soil of receptivity for what we hope to do. This may mean that the first time a church group requests our services,

[1] Austin C. Lovelace and William C. Rice, *Music and Worship in the Church* (Nashville: Abingdon Press, 1960), p. 154.

we will begin by singing with them the very song they like best. But, of course, we will not stop there. We will then go on to present in the most interesting way we know one of the great hymns of the church that all should know and love. The first psychological imperative is to meet people at their present level so that gradually they may be led to higher levels of appreciation and practice.

A second principle is equally important. We must be just as enthusiastic about the great hymns as our people are about the songs they like and use. I submit that it is because great hymns are seldom studied and sung with enthusiasm that laymen sometimes assume them to be staid, stiff, and dry. True, great hymns do not usually thrill us or touch us at their first hearing. They are not pretty in the sense that their melodies are lush and sentimental. These facts place upon those who teach the responsibility to motivate and sustain interest in these hymns until they finally win their way into the affections of our people.

Central Message of the Text

Perhaps failure to deal with the central message of hymns is responsible for the indifference and hostility so often encountered when new hymns are sung. If, when the hymn is introduced, attention is called to the great truth it contains, the hymn will receive a more sympathetic response.

The incorrect use of "Break Thou the Bread of Life" as a communion hymn illustrates our common failure at this point. A thoughtful reading of this text clearly indicates that the biblical reference is to Christ's feeding of the multitude. The hymn implies that Christ feeds us in two ways—through "the sacred page" and as "the living Word." The "bread of life" cannot be interpreted as referring to the Eucharist, for in the latter we are not fed by him but partake of the elements in memory of his life and death.

Summarizing the central message of a hymn leads to the kind of understanding that will save us from such false interpretations. Also, it will quickly expose inferior songs that have nothing worthwhile to say, just as it will call attention to the merits of hymns of quality.

Let us attempt to examine North's "Where Cross the Crowded Ways of Life," a hymn which, though widely used, is not wholly appreciated until one knows the setting out of which it was produced. A statement such as the following can strengthen the impact of this hymn upon the worshipers:

This hymn by Frank Mason North introduced a new concern for home missions. Before his day missionary hymns dealt with telling the story of Jesus to benighted heathens in foreign lands. When in 1903 North was asked to write a hymn on missions for the new *Methodist Hymnal,* the hymnal committee probably expected another text similar to "From Greenland's Icy Mountains." If so, they must have been disappointed. Looking out from his office in downtown New York, North became aware of the need for an enlightened missionary thrust right in the shadow of his own place of employment. He knew the tragedy and loneliness that stalked the great impersonal city. He knew that the message of Christ needed to be heard just as surely in the "city's streets" as in far-off lands.

After introducing his theme in stanza 1, he sets out in stanza 2 to detail in highly expressive language the unpleasant aspects of inner-city life: "crowded ways of life," "cries of race and clan," "noise of selfish strife," "haunts of wretchedness and greed," "thresholds dark with fears," and "paths where hide the lures of greed." In stanza 3 he affirms Christ's concern for "tender childhood's helplessness," "woman's grief," and "man's burdened toil." That we can become partners with Christ in deeds of loving service is the message of stanza 4, for Christ must depend on us to give "the cup of water" that "still holds the freshness of Thy grace." Stanzas 5 and 6 comprise a prayer of petition. Since these two stanzas are a single sentence, there should be only a very slight pause between them and neither should be omitted when the hymn is used. Through ministrations of loving concern, implies the poet in these stanzas, Christ can walk the streets of New York and redeem it of its pain and grief.

> Among these restless throngs abide,
> O tread the city's streets again,
>
> Till sons of men shall learn Thy love
> And follow where Thy feet have trod.

Thought Patterns [2]

There are several ways in which the central messages of hymns are developed.

1. OBJECTIVE-SUBJECTIVE. All hymns are either objective or subjective or combinations of the two. Objectivity implies that a person or thing is the "object" of attention and concern. In Christian hymnody, God is the true object of worship. This principle is violated when an inanimate object is given this exalted status, whether it be a particular type of cross ("The Old Rugged Cross"), or a garden ("In the Garden" or "The Beautiful Garden of Prayer"), or a kind of palace ("Ivory Palaces"). Indeed these objects may be referred to in worship, but they should never become the subject of hymns, thus taking priority over God and Christ. Subjectivity implies that the focus of attention is turned upon the poet or the singer. If not controlled and dis-

---

[2] Patterns of this type were discussed by Carl F. Price in *Religion and Life*, Summer, 1947, pp. 431-42.

ciplined, subjectivity can lead to an unwholesome self-concern. As we have indicated, many gospel songs are heavily weighted on the subjective side, as a result of which their use should always be balanced with hymns of the objective, God-centered type. Testing a number of hymns for objectivity or subjectivity is a profitable project, for it will induce thoughtful reading that leads to greatly increased understanding.

Many of our very best hymns are both objective and subjective. For example, the first three stanzas of Faber's "There's a Wideness in God's Mercy" are objective—setting forth the attributes of the Eternal—while the final stanza turns the spotlight of concern on the singer:

> If our love were but more simple,
>   We should take Him at His word;
> And our lives would be all sunshine
>   In the sweetness of our Lord.

Again, in How's "O Jesus, Thou Art Standing," the first half of each stanza is addressed to Christ, whereas the latter portion expresses our subjective response:

> O Jesus, Thou art standing
>   Outside the fast-closed door,
> In lowly patience waiting
>   To pass the threshold o'er: [objective]
> Shame on us, Christian brethren,
>   His name and sign who bear;
> O shame, thrice shame upon us,
>   To keep Him standing there! [subjective]

2. HEBREW PATTERN. Closely related to the pattern just discussed is the Hebrew pattern consisting of *vision, confession,* and *elevation* or *realization.* The label derives from

Isaiah's Temple experience and from the steps through which he passed in his confrontation of the Almighty (Isaiah 6). Observe this pattern in Walter Russell Bowie's brotherhood hymn, "O Holy City, Seen of John." Note the vision of the "Holy City" in the opening stanza:

> *Vision—*
> O holy city, seen of John,
>   Where Christ, the Lamb, doth reign,
> Within whose foursquare walls shall come
>   No night, nor need, nor pain,
> And where the tears are wiped from eyes
>   That shall not weep again!

Stanzas 2 and 3 acknowledge human responsibility for the failure of mankind to realize this vision:

> *Confession—*
> O shame to us who rest content
>   While lust and greed for gain
> In street and shop and tenement
>   Wring gold from human pain,
> And bitter lips in blind despair cry,
>   "Christ hath died in vain!"

Prayerfully and hopefully the final stanza suggests the ultimate fulfillment of the dream:

> *Realization—*
> Already in the mind of God
>   That city riseth fair:
> Lo, how its splendor challenges
>   The souls that greatly dare—
> Yea, bids us seize the whole of life
>   And build its glory there.[3]

[3] Used by permission of Harper & Row, Publishers.

3. TRINITARIAN PATTERN. Far more obvious is the trinitarian formula, in which each person of the Trinity is made the subject of one stanza. In "Come, thou Almighty King" stanzas 1, 2, and 3 deal with the "Almighty King," the "Incarnate Word," and the "Holy Comforter" respectively, while stanza 4 is a summary ascription of praise to the "great One in Three." In William C. Doane's "Ancient of Days," stanza 1 is directed to the "Ancient of Days," an Old Testament title for God; stanzas 2, 3, and 4 are addressed to "O Holy Father," "O Holy Jesus," and "O Holy Ghost" respectively. The final stanza voices the synthesis in the ascription to "O Triune God."

4. PARADOX AND CONTRAST. The use of paradox and contrast to communicate great ideas is widespread in our hymnody. This is not strange, because there are many paradoxes implicit in the Christian faith, the chief of which was the main burden of Jesus' message, namely, that he who would save his life must be willing to lose it for the sake of the gospel, and that he who would be the master must be the servant of all (Matthew 16:25; 20:26). Harry Webb Farrington's "I Know Not How That Bethlehem's Babe" typifies this pattern through the use of "I know not" and "I only know" in each of its stanzas.

> I know not how that Bethlehem's Babe
> Could in the Godhead be;
> I only know the manger Child
> Has brought God's life to me.[4]

Perhaps the most outstanding example of a hymn built on the idea of paradox is George Matthesons's "Make Me a Captive, Lord." The author, with effective symbolism, maintains

[4] Copyright by Harry Webb Farrington; used by permission of the Hymn Society of America.

that freedom cannot be won except by the true disciple who is taken captive by the Master.

> Make me a captive, Lord,
>   And then I shall be free;
> Force me to render up my sword,
>   And I shall conqueror be.

Literary Patterns

Devices employed by hymn-text authors with regard to poetic structure can be of real interest to the student of hymnody, though they often go unnoticed and unappreciated by ministers and laymen. An imaginative pattern does not insure a great hymn. In fact, an obvious pattern at times may disguise the lack of real worth, the pattern serving as a coverup for mediocrity of message. When the content and language of a hymn are otherwise commendable, however, textual patterns add interest and motivate usage.

1. CONVERSATIONAL. Hymns marked by this pattern are adaptable for use as hymn anthems in that the lines of conversation may be sung by different sections or solo voices in various combinations. Impressive when treated in this manner is John M. Neale's setting of the early Greek hymn, variously translated as "Art Thou Weary, Art Thou Troubled," or "Art Thou Weary, Art Thou Languid." A. E. Bailey's imaginative and colorful picture as to how this hymn may have been originally conceived will enhance its interest and value.[5] After an introductory stanza in which Jesus' invitation is suggested, subsequent stanzas consist of a series of questions and answers, the former posed by a seeker who has heard of the faith of this band of early

---
[5] A. E. Bailey, *The Gospel in Hymns* (New York: Charles Scribner's Sons, 1950), pp. 290-91.

Christians and wants to know more about it, the answers provided by one who holds the faith and witnesses to its power.

> *Seeker*—
> Hath He marks to lead me to Him,
> If He be my guide?
> *Christian witness*—
> In His feet and hands are woundprints,
> And His side.
>
> *Seeker*—
> If I ask Him to receive me,
> Will He say me nay?
> *Christian witness*—
> Not till earth and not till heaven
> Pass away.

2. ITEMIZATION. The splendid hymn by Wilbur Fisk Tillett, "O Son of God Incarnate," illustrates the literary device of itemization. In this instance there is double use of the device in that the opening lines of the four stanzas are balanced by complementing lines as follows:

Opening lines	*Fifth lines*
O Son of God Incarnate,	God's light to earth Thou bringest
O Mind of God incarnate,	God's thought to earth Thou bringest
O Heart of God incarnate,	God's love to earth Thou bringest
O Will of God incarnate.	God's will to earth Thou bringest

In Bernard Barton's "Walk in the Light" the four stanzas are built on the verbs or actions that will result to him who follows the injunction in the title. Following the identical opening line in each stanza, the text is developed as follows:

Stanza 1—
   . . . so shalt thou *know*
   That fellowship of love.

Stanza 2—
   . . . and thou shalt *find*
   Thy heart made truly His.

Stanza 3—
   . . . and thou shalt *own*
   Thy darkness passed away.

Stanza 4—
   . . . and thine shall *be*
   A path, though thorny, bright.

At times the itemization is not as apparent as in the examples just cited. Georgia Harkness's hymn, "Hope of the World," which embraces both personal devotion and social concern, is somewhat more subtle in its textual arrangement.

Hope of the world, thou Christ of great compassion,
   Speak to our fearful hearts by conflict rent;
Save us, thy people, from consuming passion,
   Who by our own false hopes and aims are spent.

Hope of the world, God's gift from highest heaven,
   Bringing to hungry souls the bread of life,
Still let thy spirit unto us be given
   To heal earth's wounds and heal her bitter strife.

Hope of the world, afoot on dusty highways,
   Showing to wandering souls the path of light;
Walk thou beside us lest the tempting byways
   Lure us away from thee to endless night.[6]

---

[6] From *Eleven Ecumenical Hymns*, copyright 1954 by The Hymn Society of America; used by permission.

Reduced to its barest outline, this hymn, addressed to Christ, expresses the prayer that he may *speak, save, feed, heal, show,* and *walk*. Only by careful analysis will the full meaning of this hymn become vivid and clear. Of recent composition, it deserves careful presentation in these years during which congregations are being introduced to it.

For a final example, consider the splendid hymn of praise, "Crown Him With Many Crowns," in which stanzas 2, 3, and 4 name Christ the Lord of *life, peace,* and *love* respectively.

3. LITANY. Prayer hymns to which a response is added are thereby cast in the form of a litany. Such hymns are easily adapted to solo-choir or choir-congregation usage. For example, "For the Beauty of the Earth" may be treated in this fashion; a soloist or solo section sings the stanzas, the choir responding with the ascription:

> Lord of all, to Thee we raise
> This our hymn of grateful praise.

Or the choir may sing the stanzas, the congregation responding on the final refrain. The hymn "Rejoice, Ye Pure in Heart," although not a prayer and therefore not, strictly speaking, a litany can also be sung in responsive fashion, a small group singing the stanzas and the larger ensemble joining on the refrain. Similar treatment can be given the favorite Advent hymn, "O Come, O Come, Immanuel," in which the stanzas should be sung in unison and the refrain in harmony.

Unique Musical Fitness

The tune is intended to transport the text and should not receive too much attention for its own sake; however, when the tune expresses in an unusually fine way the mood of the text, this happy circumstance should be noted. As an example, let us observe several ways in which the "Passion Chorale" augments the feeling implicit in the text, "O Sacred Head, Now Wounded." You will recall that in its original form this tune was set to a German love song and employed an entirely different rhythmic and harmonic pattern.[7] For the intensely devotional setting now in use in most hymnals we are indebted to Johann Sebastian Bach. First, note several highly expressive facets of the tune itself. The generally descending direction communicates a sense of tender sadness. The use of *mi* (the third degree of the scale) for the final tone of the hymn also contributes to its quiet, plaintive mood.

The rhythm also is uniquely appropriate. While some

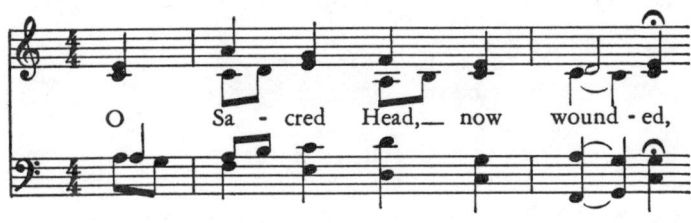

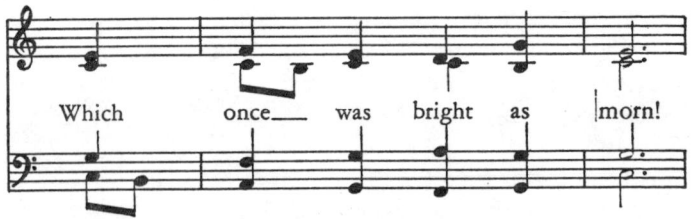

[7] For the tune in its original form see Routley, *op. cit.*

German hymns may have suffered from the evening out of the time values, in this instance a return to Hassler's rhythms would introduce a kind of excitement that would destroy the desired mood. Note that the only half notes in the hymn tune occur on poignant, expressive syllables—the very syllables that would be sustained in expressive reading. Not only is expressiveness evident in the tune, it is even more apparent in Bach's inspired harmonization. For purposes of study, isolate the harmonic cadence that closes each phrase, observing how the harmonic progressions move from dissonance to consonance to enhance the moods of such words as *wounded, suffered, sorrow, anguish,* and *languish.* Again, observe that the most biting dissonance in

the entire hymn occurs between *e* and *f* in the soprano and alto lines on the word *abuse.* We cannot claim that this tone painting was intentional, for the concepts of the German hymn for which Bach provided this harmonization are not identical with our translation "O Sacred Head." But this fact does not diminish the effectiveness of the text-tune combination and should not prevent us from noting it in our use of the hymn.

Specific Musical Features

Because the average person is not as observant of the music as of the text, musical features are seldom apparent to him unless revealed through study. These features, when exposed, become a means of motivating interest in a hymn and offer a device for the teaching of it. In this brief discussion we wish to mention and illustrate five of the most common musical features of hymn tunes.

1. SONG FORM. If music is to have quality, it must satisfy the requirements of good form. Although form in music is a large and involved subject, for our purposes in treating hymn tunes it is enough to acknowledge the importance of two factors—unity and variety. Unity is secured through repetition, either of entire musical phrases, or of specific rhythmic or melodic note groups. Variety is secured through contrast or change. In many hymn tunes the opening melodic phrase is repeated immediately or is restated later following contrasting material. A tune involving *statement, contrast,* and *restatement* is cast in the ABA form.[8] In the familiar Beethoven tune used with "Joyful, Joyful, We Adore Thee," the first, second, and fourth lines are identical and the contrast occurs in the third phrase; thus the form is AABA. This tune is as unified as a tune can be. On the other hand, there are tunes that have no exact repetition of melodic phrases. The familiar Netherlands "Hymn of Thanksgiving" is a case in point, and its form would have to be labeled ABCD. There is unity and coherence in this tune, but it is rhythmic rather than melodic. Tapping the rhythm will reveal this clearly.

BETWEEN THE relative simplicity of AABA and the intricacy of ABCD there are many other forms, several of which we shall list here, together with hymn tune examples:

---

[8] For further explanation of song form in language understandable to the musical layman, see Sigmund Spaeth, *The Art of Enjoying Music* (New York: McGraw-Hill Book Co., Inc., 1933), pp. 93 ff.

AABA

Come Thou Fount (Nettleton)
O Master Workman (St. Michel's)

AABCD

Praise to the Lord (Lobe den Herren)
He Who Would Valiant Be (St. Dunstan's)
Sing Praise to God (Mit Freuden zart)

AABBCCDDEEF

All Creatures of Our God and King (Lasst uns erfreuen)

ABABCD

I Look to Thee (O Jesu)
If Thou But Suffer God (Neumark)

ABBA

For the Might of Thine Arm (Cormac)

2. REPETITION. As we have seen, the majority of hymn tunes employ repetition, either of entire phrases or of rhythmic or melodic fragments. For example, "Lasst uns erfreuen," listed above as AABBCCDDEEF is clearly an *echo* tune. By the use of the echo or antiphonal approach, it can be taught in its entirety the very first time the hymn is attempted. The leader should inform the group of this feature, instructing them to be attentive to each line when sung by the choir, since they will sing the same melody immediately after they have heard it, though of course to different words. After the five repeated motifs have been sung, one "Alleluia" will be left over.

In the hymn "Praise to the Lord, the Almighty" the first phrase is repeated in exact imitation, after which three additional motifs occur; and in "St. Michel's," to which Jay T. Stocking's "O Master Workman of the Race" is set, the fourth score of the music repeats the second score. From these examples it can be seen that many of our hymns secure musical unity with repetition. The leader of hymn singing will call attention to repetition in his teaching procedures.

3. MELODIC SEQUENCES. Where a melodic fragment or group of notes is repeated at a different pitch level, we have what may be termed a sequential pattern. Here too, learning is facilitated if the sequential pattern is recognized. Moreover, the sequence frequently will add to the cumulative emotional effect of the text, especially when the text calls for progress toward a climax. McCutchan's setting of "Let All the World in Every Corner Sing" offers an excellent example of sequential patterns that seem absolutely correct as a means of expressing the mood of the text.[9] The melodic fragment over the words "The heavens are not too high" recurs one step higher over "His praise may thither fly," another step higher on "The earth is not too low," and one step higher still on "His praises there must grow." The cumulative effect of this little melody sung at four successive higher pitch levels is such that a tremendous climax is felt on the final:

> Let all the world in every corner sing:
> My God and King!

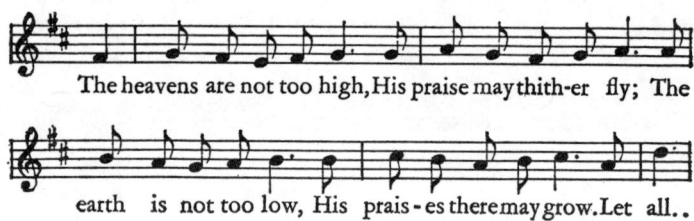

From The Methodist Hymnal. Music copyright renewal 1962, assigned to Abingdon Press.

The effective use of sequence within a single musical phrase may be found in certain of the strong Welsh hymn

[9] John Porter, listed as the composer of "All the World," was the penname for Robert Guy McCutchan.

tunes. In "Joanna," set to "Immortal, Invisible, God Only Wise," the first two intervals are repeated immediately one step higher. This sequence, repeated in the second line and altered in the fourth, is the tune's most distinctive feature.

"Ton-Y-Botel" (or "Ebenezer"), set to "Once to Every Man and Nation," is characterized by a three-tiered pattern in the first, second, and third measures of the opening score. Because three of the four scores of this tune are identical, the tune derives much of its character from the sequences. Considered by some to be a difficult tune to sing, I submit that much of the difficulty would melt away if, in the first encounter with it, the sequential pattern were spotted and exploited.

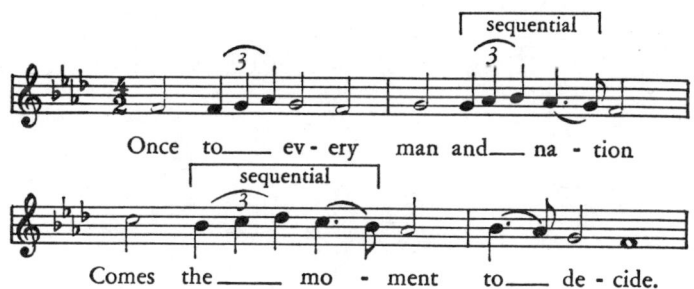

4. RELATION OF MELODIC STYLE TO MOOD OF TEXT. Hymns of praise and adoration are frequently wedded to tunes that

use melodic skips rather than stepwise patterns. Note the number of skips in "Come, thou Almighty King" and observe their majestic effect.

Subjective and meditative hymns tend to call on short-ranged tunes. The tune "Rest," set to John Greenleaf Whittier's "Dear Lord and Father of Mankind," furnishes our example. This tune has few large skips and its range is limited to an octave. The mood of prayerful humiliation is surely attained in this text-tune combination.

Copyright. By permission of The Psalms and Hymns Trust.

Another splendid example is "Redhead No. 76"—an especially moving and appropriate tune for the subjective passion hymn "Go to Dark Gethsemane." The range is less than an octave and there are no large intervals. It is a selfless tune that speaks simply and eloquently, but in hushed tones, of the passion of our Lord, as befits a hymn in which the third stanza closes with the prayer, "Learn of Jesus Christ to die."

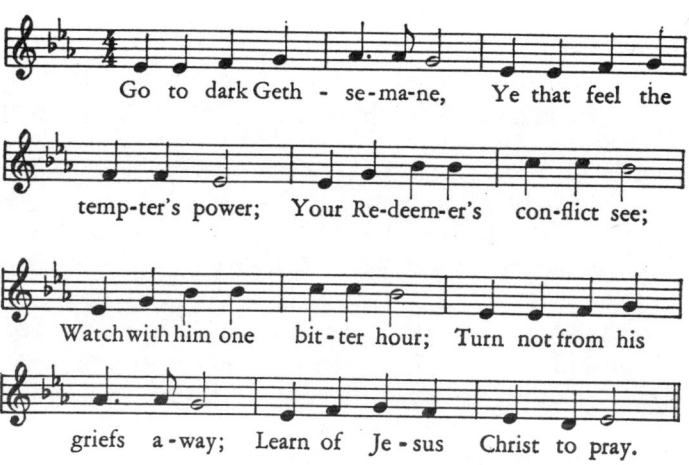

Go to dark Geth - se - ma - ne, Ye that feel the tempt-er's power; Your Re-deem-er's con-flict see; Watch with him one bit - ter hour; Turn not from his griefs a - way; Learn of Je - sus Christ to pray.

5. MINOR-MAJOR PATTERN. The average person, even though musically untrained, is able to spot and identify minor tonality in contrast to major. As most tunes are in the major mode, the occasional minor hymn provides expressive variety. Though it is well known that not all minor music is sad, just as not all major music is joyful, there is a serious and somber quality about most of the minor hymn tunes in use. For the exception we may turn to "Leoni," set to "The God of Abraham Praise," which, though minor, is as joyful as its text demands.

In a few hymn tunes, especially those of John B. Dykes, the minor-major pattern is employed to give expression to the changing moods of the texts. In "Vox Dilecti," composed especially for "I Heard the Voice of Jesus Say," the composer clothes Jesus' words of invitation in the minor mode, reserving the major tonality for the subjective response of the singer.

WE SHOULD remember that a particular hymn may have a number of features that are worthy of emphasis when the hymn is presented. To cover all the points of interest at the first presentation would be unwise. Rather, the leader must decide on the particular feature he wishes to highlight and reserve other points of interest for later use. Just as we need motivation to respond to new hymns, so we need to approach familiar hymns with the new enthusiasm that fresh insights will bring. It might be wise for those who teach and direct hymns to keep a notebook listing under each hymn distinctive features such as we have discussed. A record should be kept of the occasions on which the hymn was presented and the particular aspect featured, whether it be the central message; points of literary or musical beauty; or specific conceptual, literary, or musical patterns. In addition, such a notebook could also contain material concerning the author and the composer and useful anecdotes (exclusive of purely fictional hymn stories) connected with the composition and later use of the hymn.

It is hoped that the afore-mentioned ideas will help leaders move beyond "arm-waving" to hymn direction based on an adequate store of information and creative imagination.

↓ I hope so!

CHAPTER 7

Interpretation of Hymns

HYMNS ARE INTENDED TO BE SUNG. THEREFORE, HOW THE hymn is performed is just as important as the internal quality of the hymn itself. Obviously our ultimate goal in hymn singing is reached when a great hymn is performed accurately and interpreted thoughtfully.

Accuracy of Performance
"Sing them exactly as they are printed here, without altering or mending them." [1]

Hymns should be played and sung accurately. The author has heard well-meaning pianists play 3/4 hymns in 4/4 and vice versa. Some persons play all hymns in the same key, faking them of course. Others play the tune fairly accurately but cannot keep up with the left hand part, at times producing a drone bass like a Scottish bagpipe. Still others play everything in fox-trot style. So damaging are these hymn-playing aberrations that I would advise absolute note perfect performance as the minimal standard. Most errors are the result of "playing by ear." To play folk tunes and popular songs in this way may be a pleasant pastime, but the accompaniment of hymns is a serious enterprise,

[1] John Wesley's rules for singing.

demanding both intellectual and technical honesty. To play a hymn tune other than the way the composer or arranger intended is unfair both to the hymn and the composer.

At times inaccuracies are caused by inconsistencies in the tune itself. For example, in the hymn tune "Nicaea" ("Holy, Holy, Holy"), why did John B. Dykes not make the fragments excerpted below identical? Such rhythmic and melodic inconsistencies contribute little to the tune but rather prevent it from being performed accurately by most congregations.

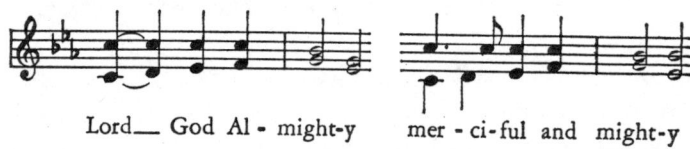

"It Came Upon the Midnight Clear" is another example of a familiar tune that is inaccurately performed. Why should the third phrase not be exactly like the first? [2] Most persons who do not read music will sing these phrases identically. Such relatively minor problems will not be overlooked by the sensitive musician, for he will approach hymn performance with a sense of integrity that will be satisfied only when complete accuracy is achieved.

Once we have become concerned about the need for correct performance, we will try to find and train leaders who can play and sing accurately. Poor musicianship becomes apparent to children and youth, and it could well

[2] *The Methodist Hymnal* (1964 edition) removes this inconsistency.

have an unfavorable effect on their attitudes toward the church and its program. Can any church or church school tolerate less of its musical workers than the ability and determination to play and sing the right notes? Accuracy is just as necessary now as in the days of John Wesley!

Hymn Tempos

"Sing in time . . . and take care not to sing too slow." [3]

Hymns should be performed at correct tempos. Departures from proper tempos take various forms. There is the player who has a horror of dragging; consequently he races through the hymns, leaving the congregation breathless in their effort to keep pace. Then there is the conscientious person who tries to play every note correctly but in so doing finds it necessary to play the hymn too deliberately. The chief basis on which to determine the correct tempo of a hymn is the ability of the congregation to sing most of the phrases in a single breath. Nothing will result in thoughtless and lifeless singing quite so quickly as tempos so slow that the singer must breathe several times within what should be a unified phrase. Because the chief appeal of inferior religious music is its movement, perhaps finding the correct tempos for great hymns will be a powerful weapon in the battle for improved standards.

Subjective prayer hymns are the ones usually sung and played at unfortunately slow tempos. We err when we equate prayerfulness with inactivity and dullness. "Spirit of God, Descend Upon My Heart," for instance, is one of the most exciting and thrilling of hymns. How can we determine the proper tempo for it? A reading of the text reveals that the lines are made up of ten syllables each, and that in certain

[3] Wesley, *op. cit.*

instances there should be no interruption for breathing within these lines. For example, phrases like "teach me to feel that Thou art always nigh," and "the kindling of the heaven-descended dove" should be sung in one breath. To make this possible, it is desirable to think of the time signature as 2/2 rather than 4/4. Since there are no eighth- or sixteenth-notes in the entire tune, this virtual doubling of the speed can be accomplished without causing difficulty for the player or singer. The performer should be sure to maintain the prayerful character of the hymn in spite of the faster tempo.

Another prayer hymn frequently sung too slowly is "O Master, Let Me Walk With Thee." If this hymn is to be meaningfully interpreted, dotted half notes rather than quarter notes must be the rhythmic unit; that is, there must be one deliberate pulse to each measure, rather than three. In performing 3/4 tunes at this faster pace, attention to mood is especially essential. Without reverent treatment 3/4 tunes can easily become "religious waltzes."

Proper Interpretation Through Phrasing

> *"Attend strictly to the sense of what you sing, and see that your heart is not carried away with the sound, but offered to God continually."* [4]

The accurate performance of hymns at an appropriate tempo will prepare the way for the next step, namely, correct phrasing. What does this term mean and what are its implications? While understanding individual words in a text is basic, real interpretation requires that attention be given to entire phrases; important words and syllables must receive proper stress in relation to the unaccented ones.

Just as in words certain syllables are stressed, so in the

[4] *Ibid.*

language of music certain pulses are stressed over others. In 4/4 meter the first beat in each measure receives the primary accent with a secondary accent on beat three, beats two and four remaining unaccented. In three-beat measures, the accent is on beat one, beats two and three remaining unaccented. The ideal hymn is one in which word accents and musical accents agree. In such cases phrasing is relatively simple.

For example, consider the hymn "Joyful, Joyful, We Adore Thee." Notice how, for the most part, only important syllables occur on strong musical pulses. Beethoven's "Hymn to Joy" is an ideal tune for this text. Indeed, van Dyke wrote the words with this tune in mind. Now suppose the performer is indifferent to meter and accent and emphasis and simply plows through the tune, singing or playing every tone and syllable with equal stress. The result is not very exciting—not at all like the sound of this same melody in Beethoven's *Ninth Symphony*. Instead sing the words with the same stress and nuance that you would employ if speaking them conversationally. When we succeed in singing as we speak, the result will be:

> Joy-ful, joy-ful, WE a-DORE thee
> GOD of GLO ry, LORD of LOVE.[5]

This kind of intelligent treatment of phrases helps recreate the ideas and feelings the hymn contains.

Even in a good hymn, there will be occasional instances of an unimportant syllable falling on a musical accent. These pose a challenge to the performer. In "Joyful, Joyful, We Adore Thee," stanza 1, there are only three relatively unimportant words on primary or secondary accents: *to, of,* and *with,* all of which occur on the third beat of the measure,

[5] From *The Poems of Henry van Dyke* (Charles Scribner's Sons, 1911).

which normally receives a secondary accent. The interpreter, as he plays or sings, should carefully avoid stressing the third beats in these measures in order to keep the word relationships appropriate. Accordingly, the first phrase in question should be stressed: "OPEN-ing to the SUN a-BOVE" rather than "OPEN-ing TO the SUN a-BOVE."[6]

Another familiar hymn in which intelligent stressing is required is "For the Beauty of the Earth." The problem is immediately apparent. When sung to the commonly used tune, "Dix," the first word *for* falls on the primary musical accent; however, a preposition should never be accented. In cases like this, the musical accent should be subordinated so that the meaning of the text will be fully realized. "FOR the BEAU-ty OF the EARTH" in singing or speaking would be unintelligent interpretation. Rather, the sensitive performer will phrase it as follows: "For the BEAU-ty of the EARTH." He will be extremely careful to avoid too much emphasis on the word *of*, which happens to be placed on the highest pitch of the first line.

It is even more difficult for the keyboard performer than for the singer to phrase correctly. To do so he must learn to think vocally as he plays. In other words he must "play the text," stanza by stanza, thus guiding the congregation in correct phrasing and thoughtful interpretation. In "Spirit of God, Descend Upon My Heart," no two stanzas will be interpreted identically. Look at the third line of each of the first three stanzas and notice how the phrasing must be altered in order to lead the congregation in correct performance.

"Playing the text" is especially important in *irregular* hymns. The classic example is "O Come, All Ye Faithful." The pickup fourth-beat chord with which this carol begins is played only on the first stanza, for the second and third

[6] *Ibid.*

stanzas do not have word equivalents to *O* in the opening line. Our hymnody is sprinkled with just enough hymns of this type to keep organists and pianists alert. Only by following the text can accompanists play with understanding.

Intelligent hymn interpretation demands continuous attention to details of this kind. Even the most familiar hymn may become more meaningful as a result of an enlightened approach in tempo and phrasing. In fact, the most-used hymns often are interpreted most poorly, possibly because they are sung so often. If hymns merit a worthy place in human experience and in divine worship, we cannot afford to be less than diligent in observing careful phrasing.

Interpretation Through Mood

"Above all, sing spiritually. Have an eye to God in every word you sing." [7]

When the thought of a hymn has been comprehended through proper phrasing, the next objective is to capture its *moods* or *feelings*. If this is to be done, directors and organists must themselves experience these religious emotions. Some leaders are quite proficient in the techniques of music but are confused and embarrassed when mention is made of the spiritual implications of their work. He who would deal meaningfully with hymns as spiritual agents in the lives of others must know in his own life the meaning of adoration, penitence, consecration, and of the other moods and feelings that are a part of Christian experience. When we recognize the mood of a hymn, we will know how to play and sing and direct it so that the mood will be recreated for all who sing it.

Let us apply this principle to one of the most challenging of the nineteenth-century hymns, James Russell Lowell's

[7] Wesley, *op. cit.*

"Once to Every Man and Nation" as sung to "Ebenezer" ("Ton-Y-Botel"). What effect will discovery of the hymn's mood have on interpretation? Let us see. A thoughtful reading of the text reveals that we are dealing in this hymn with the *ultimate decision*, with the need for taking a stand. We as nations and individuals cannot continue sitting on the fence with regard to moral and ethical values. We cannot go through life evading decisions between right and wrong, motivated only by expediency.

> Once to every MAN and NATION
>   Comes the moment to DECIDE,
> In the STRIFE of TRUTH with FALSEHOOD,
>   For the GOOD or EVIL side;
> Some great cause, God's new Messiah
>   Offering each the BLOOM or BLIGHT,
> And the choice goes by forever
>   'Twixt that DARKNESS and that LIGHT.

Strength of character is required, says the author, for the right decision will not necessarily lead to fame and profit.

> Then to side with TRUTH is noble,
>   When we share her wretched crust,
> Ere her cause bring fame and profit,
>   And 'tis prosperous to be just;
> Then it is the BRAVE man chooses
>   While the COWARD stands aside,
> Till the multitude make virtue
>   Of the faith they had denied.

The capitalized words dramatize the conflict posed in the first two stanzas. The sturdy Welsh tune with its heavy tread, its uphill melodic sequences, and the relentless repetition of the group of triplets is a perfect vehicle to express the tensions, the conflicts, and the climax of a moment of decision. To recreate the mood, the tune should be played and sung firmly, in absolutely strict rhythm, with each note of the triplets carefully sounded and each beat suggesting a forward step as "man and nation" move on to the moment of decision. Surely when the mood of this hymn is recognized, its interpretation will never be casual and commonplace.

For purpose of contrast, we shall suggest appropriate moods for several additional hymns. One of the fine text-tune combinations of the last half century is Caroline Noel's "At the Name of Jesus" and R. Vaughan Williams' tune, "King's Weston":

In all the stanzas of this hymn text the mood is joyous and confident, expressing faith in a triumphant Jesus, who was, and is, and will be, the *Lord* of life. There is no tension,

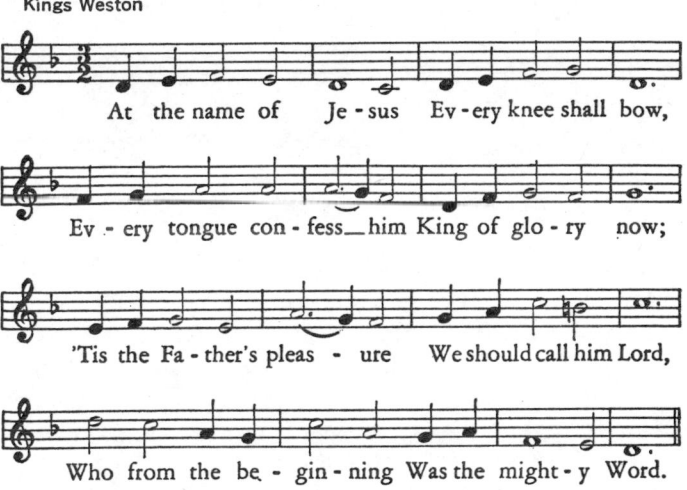

Music by R. Vaughan Williams (1872-1958). Copyright. Reprinted from *Enlarged Songs of Praise* by permission of Oxford University Press.

no conflict. Therefore, the tune should move with buoyancy and at a tempo which permits the long phrases to be sung in single breaths. Little dynamic variety (loud or soft) is called for. The necessary expression seems to be built right into the tune itself. To put it simply, this is a hymn that "sings itself."

Far more subjective is the hymn "Lord Jesus, Think On Me," set to "Southwell." This is a prayer of petition for Christ's presence in the face of sin, pain, and perplexity. It should be sung reverently, with quiet fervency. The tempo will be relatively slow, as is appropriate for a short hymn with short phrases. Because the realization of mood depends on dynamic detail, a suggested interpretation is given.

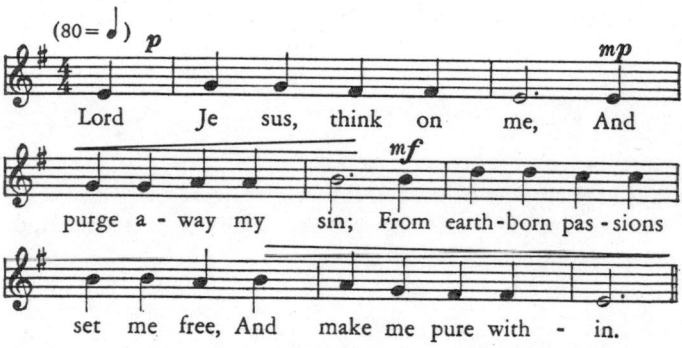

When a hymn is sung by an individual or a choir, the ultimate in expressive interpretation can be secured. When a hymn is sung by a congregation or church school assembly, the interpretation will be broad and general. If led by a sensitive, concerned director or by a well-trained choir or by an organist or pianist who interprets out of personal experience, congregational hymn singing can be far more expressive than it usually is.

How will this improvement be gained? The director will

have predetermined the pace, the phrasing, and the mood. If he directs manually, the extent and style of hand movement will vary with the mood, being more vigorous and expansive for such moods as *praise* and *adoration* and more confined for moods of *consecration* and *penitence*. His facial expression and his posture will also be agents of communication. When there are changes of mood within a given hymn, the director will convey these through visual means.

The organist and to a lesser extent the pianist have instrumental means available to suggest the mood. A hymn of praise will be stated with a fuller ensemble or on the piano with a heavier touch than a meditative prayer hymn. Furthermore, the organist has the prerogative of selecting registration according to the mood of the hymn, reserving the loudest stops (reeds and big mixtures) for hymns of praise.

The choir can assist in this interpretative effort only to the extent that it has been trained by the director to do so. When hymns are rehearsed so that organist and choir cooperate in recreating the mood, congregational singing will improve.

Terms of Expression

One more practical recommendation may be worthy of consideration. It is that we modify our vocabulary of terms of expression. Terms like louder, softer, faster, and slower do not suggest religious feelings. Try substituting for these a whole new vocabulary: majestically, humbly, triumphantly, consecratedly, and the list will grow almost without end, embracing the whole gamut of Christian attitudes and feelings.

Variety in Hymn Interpretation

It is possible to expect too much variety in congregational hymn singing. Changing organ registrations several times within a stanza and making use of the swell or crescendo pedals should be avoided. Too much ill-conceived change of registration detracts from meaningful congregational singing rather than aiding it. The organist should do only what will encourage full participation, avoiding the sudden shifts that cause consternation and confusion to the congregation. Even the most prayerful hymn should be played with a fairly full ensemble, the chief difference between it and the hymn of praise being that in the former reeds, mixtures, and the most intense principals may be taken off. In no case should congregational hymn singing be accompanied by célestes or with tremolos.

A resourceful accompanist who possesses the necessary musical skills and the taste to employ these skills with discretion may occasionally enrich certain hymns by the use of the following devices: (*a*) raising the pitch on the final stanza of a hymn of praise (in most cases it is better to pitch the earlier stanzas in a lower key, reserving the hymnal key for the final stanza), (*b*) using a descant on the final stanza, sung by a soloist, the soprano section, or played on a distinctive organ stop, (*c*) free accompaniment on final stanza with choir and congregation singing the melody in unison.

It is well to reserve this kind of treatment for a relatively small number of hymns. The use of descants and free accompaniments will depend on their availability or on the ability of the organist to improvise or compose them. Hymns like "Holy, Holy, Holy" and "For the Beauty of the Earth" are well suited to raising the key of the final stanza. This can be accomplished rather simply by playing the first three stanzas in the key of *e*-flat (three flats) for "Nicaea" and *a*-flat (four flats) for "Dix" then moving by a simple modulation to the higher key in which the hymn is usually written. In the case of "Nicaea," the modulation may be:

Mention should be made of the use of selected stanzas. It is easy to thoughtlessly ask the group to sing the first, second, and last stanzas of hymns without proper attention to what the omission of certain stanzas does to the message. Many hymns are so constructed that the singing of all the stanzas is mandatory. In others each stanza is independent of the others, so that omitting stanzas does not cause discontinuity of thought. Naturally in hymns such as "Come, thou Almighty King," in which each stanza deals with one person of the Trinity, no stanzas should be omitted. On the other hand, "For the Beauty of the Earth" is a hymn of gratitude and praise in which each stanza is complete within itself.

Is it necessary to emphasize the importance of taste and judgment in the matter of hymn interpretation? The notes and rhythms are absolute; they will be performed either correctly or incorrectly. The other matters, being somewhat subjective and relative, are not easy to explain. Perhaps we have at least encouraged the reader to consider every hymn as a possible encounter with God, and, as such, worthy of his most prayerful and careful interpretation.

CHAPTER 8

Understanding and Using The Hymnal

THIS CHAPTER IS INTENDED TO CLARIFY THE ARRANGEMENT OF the hymnal, to explain the symbols used therein, and in general to make it a more useful asset. James R. Sydnor succinctly defines a hymnal as "an anthology of hymns, to be used privately or publicly for devotional purposes by Christians."[1] While this is a simple, adequate definition, it does not follow that a hymnal is a simple book, put together casually without form and plan.

Before exploring a characteristic hymnal, a word should be said concerning the "authority of the denominational hymnal." A recent questionnaire circulated by one of the major Protestant denominations revealed that a substantial number of individual churches in that group do not use their denominational hymnal. The reason usually given was that the hymns were unknown or that they were not what the people wanted to sing. We doubt the validity of this reason for refusing to use denominational material. When through the centuries devout and learned men of God have developed translations of the Bible, has anyone the temerity to say, "We will not use this book because we do not like the ideas contained in it"? While we do not claim that a

[1] *The Hymn and Congregational Singing* (Richmond: John Knox Press, 1960), p. 77.

congregational hymnal has the force of biblical canon, we do maintain that, just as sincere men of God toiled over the ancient manuscripts that culminated in our Bible, so too have large and representative bodies of the best qualified persons in denominations labored sacrificially to produce a body of hymns to serve their groups. It is unreasonable and presumptuous for any congregation within the fellowship of a major denomination to refuse to use the hymnal appointed for its use. Most denominational hymnals have a broad enough selection of hymns to serve the needs of every congregation within its membership. Contrary to some claims, hymns in denominational books are not more difficult than those in other books. What is needed is a zeal to learn the hymns found in denominational hymnals, so that the church may be strengthened in its common faith.

What does such a book contain? Immediately prior to the first hymn will usually be found the Contents of the hymnal. The so-called nonliturgical churches usually arrange their hymnals according to topics, such as worship, God, Christ, and the Holy Spirit, Holy Scriptures, Christian life, the kingdom of God on earth, and specialized hymns in varied order.

Each of the broad categories listed above may be subdivided into several categories in a topical index. For example, one hymnal lists sixty-three hymns in the "Worship" section. Of these, thirty-two have the subheading "Adoration and Praise"; eleven, "Morning"; sixteen, "Evening"; and four, "Close of Worship." Certain denominational hymnals do not list titles above hymns, since it is commonly understood that the first line and the title are identical. If in these hymnals the section headings or subheadings are centered at the top of each page, care must be taken not to mistake them for the hymn titles. The current trend seems to be to place the hymn titles over the hymns, thus avoiding this problem and making the hymns easier to find. A few moments spent in studying the table of contents of your hymnal and the way in which hymns are classified will be profitable.

Denominational hymnals almost always print authorship of the text, composer of the tune, name of the tune, and metrical scheme on the same page as the hymn itself. Generally names of authors and translators or references to the sources of hymn texts are at the reader's left, immediately above the hymn. In the case of the hymn, "Shepherd of Eager Youth," for example, we may find the following entry:

>Clement of Alexandria, c. 170-215
>Trans. by Henry M. Dexter, 1821-1890

This tells us that Clement of Alexandria, the date of whose birth was about A.D. 170 and who died in 220, was the author, and that the translation into English was made by Henry M. Dexter, who lived from 1821 to 1890. Occasionally authorship is obscure, in which case other relevant information will be given. In "The First Noel," where the author is usually listed we find "Traditional English Carol," which is as close as we can come to knowing the hymn's origin.

In the case of metrical psalm settings, one hymnal uses this form:

>From Psalm c
>Isaac Watts, 1674-1748, alt.[2]

From this we learn that this hymn is Watts's paraphrase of the one hundredth psalm, together with his dates and the

[2] "Before Jehovah's Awefull Throne."

fact that in several places Watts's setting has been altered.

Occasionally an anonymous text will be identified only by the title of a larger work of which it is a part, as when "Let All Mortal Flesh Keep Silence" is headed by "Liturgy of St. James." The student of hymns should examine all the entries given in connection with texts to make sure that he understands what they signify.

The tune name and information regarding the composer, arranger, or source of the tune is placed above the hymn on the right-hand side. An even wider variety of entries will be found here. This is quite understandable when we realize that so many hymn tunes were not composed originally for this purpose but have been borrowed from longer musical compositions. It is not unusual then to find "arr. from" as in the case of Beethoven's "Hymn to Joy," arranged from the final movement of the great master's *Ninth Symphony*. Or in the case of the folk tune "Kingsfold," the listing may be:

>Kingsfold
>Traditional English Melody
>Arr. by R. Vaughan Williams, 1872-1961

This tells us that the folk tune was arranged for the hymnal by Williams. Another familiar entry relating to the music is "adapted from." The tune "Lyons," as set to "O Worship the King," is said to be adapted from the composer Johann M. Haydn, meaning that someone (in this case Lowell Mason) selected this particular melody, probably from a longer musical work, and rearranged it as a hymn tune. Or again the familiar tune to "Hark, the Herald Angels Sing" was composed by Mendelssohn as a male-chorus composition with a secular text. It was for William H. Cummings, a noted tenor of the nineteenth century, to adapt Mendelssohn's tune for use with Charles Wesley's Christmas text.

Among the other abbreviated bits of information accompanying names of composers or sources of tunes are "melody from," implying that the harmonization has been supplied later and "harmonized by," whose meaning is self-evident.

As with texts, many tunes can be traced only to a certain collection. Before the days of copyrights and royalties, authors and composers were not always identified, so that many hymn collections were published without specific credit for each title. The result is that such a great tune as "Mit Freuden zart" can be identified only as being "From the Bohemian Brethren's *Gesangbuch*, 1566."

That a great deal of information can be packed into the brief space above each hymn is well illustrated by "O Sacred Head, Now Wounded" in which case the following may be given:

Authorship Uncertain	Passion Chorale
Tr. By Paul Gerhardt 1607-1676	Hans L. Hassler, 1564-1612
Tr. by James W. Alexander, 1804-1859	Harmonized by J. S. Bach, 1685-1750

It should be explained that the original poem was written in Latin, and that Gerhardt made the translation from Latin into German, and Alexander from German into English.

Tune Names

Many hymn texts are sung to more than one tune and many tunes serve more than one text. This flexibility makes it necessary to identify the tunes themselves; hence either above the hymn or immediately above the name of the composer will be found the tune name. The trained student of hymnody will always refer to tunes by their names rather than by the text or texts with which they may be associated. Hymns such as "All Hail the Power of Jesus' Name" and "When I Survey the Wondrous Cross" for several centuries have been sung to various tunes. In programing these hymns, it is essential to indicate the tune to be used, in the first instance "Coronation," "Miles' Lane," or "Diadem." That the second and third tunes are included not simply to fill space is borne out by the fact that in a recent denominational poll 94 per cent of the respondents indicated the occasional use of "Coronation"; 66 per cent, "Diadem"; and 57 per cent, "Miles' Lane." More than half of the churches in this denomination are familiar with and at times use each of the three tunes given. To refer to them as the first, second, and third tune does not suffice, for they are listed in varying order in different hymnals. If the student will simply be observant as he encounters various tunes, he will soon be able to identify them by their names.

A composer is, of course, free to label his tune as he chooses.[3] The following represent a cross section of the types of names that are commonly used:

"Duke Street"—the street on which the composer, John Hatton, lived

"Nicaea"—a great event, the Council of Nicaea, formulating Trinitarian doctrine dealt with in the text to which it is commonly sung

"Mendelssohn"—named for the composer

"Keble"—named for the author of the text for which it was composed

"Creation"—named for the oratorio from which it is taken

[3] Robert Guy McCutchan, hymnologist and editor of *The Methodist Hymnal*, 1935, made an exhaustive study of hymn-tune names, and the student would do well to become familiar with his book entitled, *Hymn Tune Names: Their Sources and Significance* (Nashville: Abingdon Press, 1957).

"Ein' feste Burg"—named for the first line of the hymn in the original language

Metrical Patterns

The hymn-tune name is usually followed by a series of numbers or letters that indicate the metrical pattern. The hymn "Holy, Holy, Holy" is, of course, set to "Nicaea," after which the numbers 11. 12. 12. 10 appear. These digits indicate the number of lines in the hymn and the number of syllables in each of the lines. This hymn consists of four lines, which in turn are made up of eleven, twelve, twelve, and ten syllables respectively.

If we could assume that every congregation were able to sing successfully every tune to every hymn text that the pastor or worship leader might select, there would be no value in learning about metrical patterns. This, however, is not often the case. The purpose of learning the meaning of the numerals comprising the metrical scheme is that by so doing it becomes possible to substitute for an unknown or an unsingable tune one that will fit the text and be familiar to the group.

For a practice project, select a hymn that is not used widely, possibly because of a dull or unsingable tune—for example, Wilbur Fisk Tillett's "O Son of God Incarnate." [4]

> O Son of God incarnate,
> O Son of man divine!
> In whom God's glory dwelleth,
> In whom man's virtues shine;
> God's light to earth Thou bringest
> To drive sin's night away,
> And through Thy life, so radiant,
> Earth's darkness turns to day.

[4] The reference is to the tune "Incarnation." *The Methodist Hymnal* (1964 edition) uses the singable and interesting tune "Far Off Lands."

Elementary arithmetic reveals that this hymn consists of eight lines with the following syllable count: 7. 6. 7. 6. 7. 6. 7. 6. Actually the pattern may be set down as 7. 6. 7. 6. D., the letter *D* indicating the repetition of the first four lines. Now turn to the metrical index of tunes and find the list under 7. 6. 7. 6. D. As this is a frequently used metrical pattern, there will be considerable choice. On what basis shall an alternate tune be selected? Certainly it should be familiar—so familiar that the group can sing it without having to turn back and forth from the text to the tune. Second, the general spirit of the tune should agree with the mood of the text. Some 7. 6. 7. 6. D. tunes are marked by joyousness, others are contemplative and restful. Obviously we should not select a tune that suggests the opposite mood from that of the text. Third, textual and musical accents should agree. This is especially important in the case of the 7. 6. 7. 6. D. pattern, for in some poems in this meter the first word in each line and alternate syllables thereafter are stressed, as in "RISE, my SOUL, and STRETCH thy WINGS." In other 7. 6. 7. 6. D. hymns, such as "O Jesus, THOU art STANDing," the second, fourth, and sixth syllables are accented. For a hymn text in the latter category, a tune must be chosen that will begin with an upbeat in order that the musical accents occur simultaneously with those of the text.

On the basis of these qualities, which tune shall we select for "O Son of God Incarnate"? We will immediately exclude "Llangloffan" and "Ellon" as they are not any better known than the tune we are trying to replace. Observing that this text is marked by an active quality as the author elicits a commitment to a life of service, we will exclude "Homeland" and the "Passion Chorale" because of their meditative and subjective character. "Work Song" is very well known but would be entirely unfitting because of false accents. Perhaps we will decide on "Aurelia," which is familiar, dynamic in mood, and entirely appropriate in terms of accent and stress.

A look into the past history of hymn singing will show that this procedure of fitting tunes to texts had to go on constantly because of a tune shortage. In a study of the hymns of the Schwenkfelders, a small but highly literate and cultured sect that emigrated from Germany to Pennsylvania in 1734, the author analyzed twenty-five copy books in which Schwenkfelder boys and girls transcribed the melodies to which their hymns were sung. The printed hymnbook of the group contained in excess of five hundred texts but not a single tune. The only tunes available for several decades were those found in Bohemian Brethren hymnbooks which the emigrants brought with them from their homeland. These books, actually printed in 1556, 1580, and 1609, had been in use over a hundred years before they crossed the Atlantic! In the copybooks young Schwenkfelders placed over each tune the numbers of the hymns in their printed hymnbooks that were sung to that tune. It is not uncommon to find that up to a dozen texts were sung to a given tune. In some religious groups the supply of tunes was even more limited so that it was necessary to use the few well known tunes with a wide variety of texts.

This leads us to consider the metrical patterns to which letter names are given. During the period of English hymnody in which only metrical psalms were sung in public worship, it became the practice to arrange the translations or paraphrases according to one of these patterns—short meter (6. 6. 8. 6.), common meter (8. 6. 8. 6.), or long meter (8. 8. 8. 8.).[5] The few tunes available accounted for the use of these standard patterns. Also, John Calvin insisted on simplicity in structure that would keep the hymns free from the gaudiness of folk song, and this puritanic ideal

[5] See Chapter 10 for a more detailed treatment of metrical psalmody.

prevailed in the tunes as well as in texts. Most of Isaac Watts's hymns employ one of these meters, as Watts wrote before the time when a newfound freedom opened the way for more metrical variety. In fact, Watts had a great deal to do with creating a climate in which further freedom could be realized, though it remained for Charles Wesley and later writers actually to write in the new meters.

The final category in the metrical index is labeled "Irregular." Here are the hymns in which not all stanzas have the same number of syllables. An example should clarify this. A glance at the opening words of the first and second stanzas of "O Come, All Ye Faithful" is sufficient.[6] Of course, alternate tunes cannot be substituted for such hymns; neither can irregular hymns be substituted for one another.

Indexes

Most hymnals have five or six separate indexes. All can be useful, especially to the serious student of hymnody. Many separate and rewarding projects in the study of hymns can be initiated by index research. For example, a study of the hymns by the great poets can begin with a listing of the familiar literary giants given in the index of authors, translators, and sources. In one hymnal the names of Addison, Bunyan, Byron, Holmes, Johnson, Kipling, Longfellow, Lowell, Rossetti, Tennyson, and Whittier promise a rich experience. Or again, a study of hymns based on the Psalms will begin by noting in the index the listing of these hymns together with the psalms on which they are based. This index will also reveal at a glance the prolific authors to whom we are especially indebted: Charles Wesley, Isaac Watts, James Montgomery, and the noted translator of German hymn texts, Catherine Winkworth—to name a few.

[6] See Chapter 7 for suggestions regarding the playing of irregular hymns.

The index of composers, arrangers, and sources reveals the tremendous musical debt we owe to countless composers such as J. S. Bach, Lowell Mason, and John B. Dykes from earlier centuries and R. Vaughan Williams and Martin Shaw of our own day. Here too we learn which tunes come from ancient plainsongs and which are based on early American melodies. The Welsh tunes are listed separately, as are traditional melodies and carols, and musical settings whose sources are unknown.

We should note also the alphabetical index of tunes, which will have increasing value as the student becomes accustomed to referring to hymn tunes by their names. There are times when a tune will be more memorable and of more worth than some of the texts with which it may be used. In such cases the tune can be found more quickly by referring to this index. For example, while "Commandments" is one of the most historic tunes in Protestant hymnody, at the moment I cannot recall the text to which it is set. I refer to the Index of Tunes and find that it occurs twice in the hymnal before me, being used with "Father, We Thank Thee, Who Hast Planted" and "The Day Thou Gavest, Lord, Is Ended." Also, from this index we can see at a glance the hymn tunes that are used more than once in the hymnal, noting that "Old 100th," "St. Peter," and "Stuttgart," are among the most useful tunes in our hymnody.

The topical index goes far beyond the table of contents with the assistance it provides. A hymn may be used in connection with several themes, even though it appears only once in the hymnal. The cross-referencing that calls attention to this multiple usefulness is in this index. There is an obvious danger in overdependence on this index; that is, it can easily become a crutch on which the pastor or worship leader always depends for his choices. No single topical index is absolutely complete. The very finest hymn for a given theme may not be listed under that topic. The sincere student will develop his own "built in" topical index, for he will come to know the hymnal so well that he will not have to depend entirely on this aid.

An index of first lines is contained in all hymnals. Past custom has utilized the same number for the several tunes provided for a given text. More recent hymnals provide separate numbers for each of the tunes to which a text is set. The tunes are usually located in sequence and are numbered consecutively.

Other symbols and terms in the hymnal deserve explanation. Among these are the following:

> Anonymous—unknown; used in relation to authorship or composership.
>
> Ascribed to—authorship or composership not certain, tentative only.
>
> In Unison—only the melody to be sung.
>
> Harmony—the parts to be sung; used only after a previous unison.
>
> c.—about, when referring to dates: c. 1400.
>
> d.—died, when referring to dates: Thomas Tallis, d. 1585.
>
> Attr.—attributed to.
>
> Para. by—paraphrase by.
>
> Alternative tune—at times listed beneath a particular hymn.

In addition to the main body of hymns, most denominational hymnals also contain what might be termed broadly "service music." The character of this music depends to a great extent on the worship thought and practice of the denomination. Liturgical churches make more use of chants, ancient hymns, and canticles than nonliturgical groups. The student of hymnody should develop some appreciation and working knowledge of these specialized forms of service music. Service responses need not be limited to material found in the service music section of the hymnal. Alfred Haas and Federal Lee Whittlesey have been especially helpful in pointing out hymn stanzas that are well adapted for use as service responses.[7] The following examples may serve to spur the reader to further discoveries of useful excerpts from hymns.

Introits or Choral Calls to Worship: *Tune Names:*

All People That on Earth Do Dwell
(Stanza 1) Old 100th

Jesus, Where'er Thy People Meet
(Stanza 1) Malvern, Federal Street, or Kedron

All Praise to Our Redeeming Lord
(Stanza 1) Armenia

Jesus, We Look to Thee (Stanzas 1, 4) Mornington

Choral Calls to Prayer:

If Thou But Suffer God to Guide Thee (Stanza 1) Bremen (Neumark)

Talk With Us, Lord, Thyself Reveal
(Stanza 1) Gräfenberg

Hear Our Prayer, O Lord (While generally used as a response following prayer, this has been used most effectively in some churches as an introduction to the pastoral prayer.)

[7] Mr. Haas is professor of practical theology at Drew Theological Seminary. Dr. Whittlesey formerly was minister of music at Highland Park Methodist Church, Dallas, Texas, and is the author of *A Comprehensive Program of Church Music* (Philadelphia: The Westminster Press, 1957).

UNDERSTANDING AND USING THE HYMNAL

Prayer Responses:

Jesus, United by Thy Grace (Stanza 1)	St. Agnes

Responses Before Scripture:

O Word of God Incarnate (Stanza 1)	Munich
Break Thou the Bread of Life (Stanza 1)	Bread of Life
Come, Holy Ghost, Our Hearts Inspire (Stanza 2)	Winchester Old

Responses After Scripture:

Break Thou the Bread of Life (Stanza 2)	Bread of Life
How Gentle God's Commands (Stanza 1)	Dennis
How Are Thy Servants Blest, O Lord (Stanza 1)	Caithness

Sentences Before Sermon:

Master, Speak! Thy Servant Heareth	Amen, Jesus Han Skal Raade
Break Thou the Bread of Life (Stanza 1)	Bread of Life

Choral Benedictions and Benediction Responses:

Saviour, Again to Thy Dear Name We Raise (Stanza 2)	Ellers
May the Grace of Christ Our Saviour (Stanza 1)	Stuttgart
Lord, Now Lettest Now Thy Servant(s) Depart in Peace (Stanza 1 and Amen)	Nunc Dimittis

CHAPTER 9

Hymn Services

THIS SECTION IS HEADED "HYMN SERVICES" ADVISEDLY BECAUSE there is real doubt as to the genuine value of what are commonly called "Hymn Sings." The latter are frequently little more than a hodgepodge of the hymns and songs people like to sing, conducted in a manner that parades the personality of the leader or shows off the talents of an assortment of choirs, solo performers, and instrumentalists. Hymn services, on the other hand, are so carefully planned and conducted that they become an especially fine means of realizing the value of hymn singing previously discussed and of providing a rewarding experience in worship and Christian nurture.

What is the distinguishing feature of a hymn service? When a given period of time is set aside for the singing of hymns, chosen according to a specific theme and sung with understanding and devotion, we have the makings of a hymn service. We have already dealt with selecting the three hymns that constitute the average worship service. The principles cited can be applied when choosing several hymns for a brief period of singing prior to a more formal activity. The hymns should be selected to form a meaningful unit, each one adding its own valid insight. Unity and variety should be kept in mind in choosing any group of hymns to be sung.

In an effort to produce a wide variety of types of hymn services, rather strange themes are sometimes used. It seems unwise to base a hymn service on hymns by certain authors or on tunes by certain composers or on hymns of a particular period. The focus of attention in a hymn service, if it is to achieve worship values, should be a great idea or theme rather than factual information about the hymns themselves. In planning hymn services then, we must have a major objective in mind and should not allow less important considerations to take over.

Hymns Through the Ages

With the help of the necessary historic material, such a service can show the development musically and textually that marks our hymnic heritage.[1] Represented in the service would be metrical psalms (hymns of the Bible), an early Christian hymn, a Reformation hymn, and so on. The interpretative comments that accompany the singing of the hymns should lift up one or two unique and significant contributions of that particular period to the developing faith.

Hymns of the Christian Life

This service can be formulated to include some of the steps in Christian experience. There would be hymns of praise, penitence, thanksgiving, challenge, consecration, witness, and so on. Such a service, effectively planned and conducted, can be a significant agent in deepening the commitment of those who participate.

Hymns of the Church Ecumenical

The emphasis in this service can be twofold. First, it should substantiate the true ecumenicity of Christian

---

[1] See Chapter 10 for historical information.

hymnody, revealing how the hymnal is the least denominational (next to the Bible) of all the materials used. It is quite possible that in a typical Sunday service each hymn sung will represent a different denominational tradition. We may begin with a great Lutheran hymn, such as "Now Thank We All Our God." The prayer hymn could well be Quaker Whittier's "Dear Lord and Father of Mankind." The hymn of dedication may be Congregationalist S. Ralph Harlow's "O Young and Fearless Prophet." The reality of this ecumenicity of the hymnal needs to be brought home to our people, both as evidence of what has already been done, and as a symbol of the deepening unity that the church so sorely needs in this day.

Second, the hymns for this service should be chosen so as to lift up the finest ideas of each tradition represented in it. It would be possible to choose hymns that would provide propaganda in favor of one group over another and defeat the entire purpose of such a service.

A Hymn Service on the Historic Jesus and the Eternal Christ

Experience has shown that this is one of the most useful of all hymn service themes. It begins with the Jesus of history—his birth, his life of service, his passion, death, and resurrection. At the halfway point, the emphasis turns to the everliving Christ who calls us to lives of loving service. Not only does this service encourage the use of a wide variety of fine hymns but it has the advantage of taking the worshiper to the point of personal rededication and recommitment.

Hymns of the Wesleyan Revival

A service of this type is given below in its entirety as a prototype of the kind of hymn service that could be developed for any of the great religious movements and traditions. Our concern and interest in the ecumenical movement should not mean any decrease of our appreciation for the tremendous contributions of the separate traditions now represented in the ecumenical effort. This service then is comprised of hymns by Charles Wesley that constitute a spiritual autobiography of the "sweet singer" of Methodism.

> *Prelude*—tunes to familiar Wesley hymns
> *Choral call to worship*—"Blow Ye the Trumpet, Blow" (Stanzas 1, 2)
> *Invocation*—"Jesus, We Look to Thee"
> *Hymn of praise*—"O for a Thousand Tongues"
> *Choral prayer*—"Talk With Us, Lord"
> *Our Encounter With Christ*
>> Christ, the Lord of Life—"Rejoice the Lord Is King"
>> Christ, the Divine Shepherd—"Jesus, Lover of My Soul"
>> Christ, the Sun of Righteousness—"Christ, Whose Glory Fills the Skies"
>> Christ, who calls each man to a heartwarming experience—"Come, O Thou Traveler Unknown"
> *Offering*—choral preludes on several of the hymn tunes used in the service.
> *Our Response to Christ*
>> The Christian finds salvation—"O How Happy Are They Who the Saviour Obey"
>> The Christian moves toward perfection—"Love Divine, All Loves Excelling"
>> The Christian prays for a pure heart—"O for a Heart to Praise My God"
>> The Christian witnesses for Christ—"O Thou Who Camest From Above"
>> The Christian serves his fellowmen—"A Charge to Keep I Have"
> *Benediction*
> *Postlude*—tunes to familiar Wesley hymns

Hymns Based on the Korean Creed

This is a service in which hymns are used to affirm the principles of belief set down in the Korean Creed, written by Herbert Welch, a bishop of The Methodist Church. Prior to the singing of each hymn, the related portion of the creed may be read aloud by the leader. In several well-chosen sentences the director should point out ways in which the hymn used is expressive of each statement of the creed.

CHRISTIANITY—A SINGING FAITH

We Believe in the one God, Maker and Ruler of all things, Father of all men,
"This Is My Father's World"
the source of all goodness and beauty, all truth and love.
"Sing Praise to God Who Reigns Above"
We believe in Jesus Christ, God manifest in the flesh,
"Ye Servants of God, Your Master Proclaim"
our teacher, example, and redeemer, the Saviour of the world.
"All Hail the Power of Jesus' Name"
We believe in the Holy Spirit, God present with us for guidance, for comfort, and for strength.
"Spirit of God, Descend Upon My Heart"
We believe in the forgiveness of sins, in the life of love and prayer,
"Take Time to Be Holy"
and in grace equal to every need.
"Amazing Grace"
We believe in the Word of God contained in the Old and New Testaments as the sufficient rule both of faith and of practice.
"Break Thou the Bread of Life"
We believe in the Church as the fellowship for

worship and for service of all who are united to the living Lord.

"Glorious Things of Thee Are Spoken"

We believe in the Kingdom of God as the divine rule in human society, and in the brotherhood of man under the fatherhood of God.

"The Light of God Is Falling"

We believe in the final triumph of righteousness, and in life everlasting. AMEN.

"Lead On, O King Eternal"

At the conclusion of the service and immediately before the benediction, the complete creed may be read in unison by all.

It is hoped that the suggestions provided here will motivate pastors and musicians to greater creativity in the planning and use of hymn services. Choirs and congregations usually respond with real enthusiasm, and it behooves us to take advantage of the opportunity for meaningful worship and learning that these services afford.

CHAPTER 10

Our Heritage of Hymns

IN THIS CHAPTER WE WILL ATTEMPT TO SURVEY THE HISTORY of Christian hymnody with a brief discussion of the periods into which it is commonly divided and representative authors and hymns from each. It is hoped that this survey will motivate the reader to study more comprehensive treatments of the subject.

Hymns from the Bible

No one knows precisely how religious songs sounded in biblical times. We do know that music was an important part of Temple worship, that psalms and hymns were chanted in early Christian worship, and that Paul specifically directed the young churches to make use of "psalms and hymns and spiritual songs."[1] Lest we mistakenly assume that later musical practices existed during this period, the following facts should be kept in mind:

1. The major and minor scales, on which most current hymn tunes are based, were not considered appropriate for church use until the sixteenth century.

2. There were no keyboard instruments like the organ

---

[1] For a description of Temple music, see 1 Chronicles 15 and 16. Paul's admonition appears in Ephesians 5:19 and Colossians 3:16.

and piano. Primitive ~~plucked~~ string, wind, and percussion instruments quite unlike their modern counterparts were used.

3. Notation, the process of writing music, did not exist.

4. There was no part music. All songs were sung in unison.

5. Singing was probably little more than intoned speech, somewhat like modern choric speaking.

Biblical Songs of Ancient Israel

Important historically as early representations of Hebrew poetry are the following songs: Song of Deliverance (Exodus 15:1-21); Song of Deborah (Judges 5); Song of Hannah (1 Samuel 2:1); David's Lament over Saul and Jonathan (2 Samuel 1:19-27); and the *Tersanctus* (Three Holies) as quoted in Isaiah's vision (Isaiah 6:1-8).

Hebrew poetry reached its zenith, of course, in the Psalms. For our study, the following characteristics should be noted:

1. Psalms contain vivid figures of speech. A. R. Gordon says of Hebrew poetry: "Figure crowds upon figure; mixed metaphors are common, and hyperboles a matter of course. The Hebrew poets can quite naturally picture the floods clapping their hands, the hills singing for joy . . ." [2]

2. Psalms are not metrical but secure their rhythm by the use of parallel statements. For example, in Psalms 9:9 the same basic idea is expressed in the two parallel phrases:

> The Lord is a stronghold for the oppressed,
>   a stronghold in times of trouble.

In their biblical form psalms cannot be sung to metrical hymn tunes but must be chanted. Only a chant can accommodate a text in which the number of syllables varies from line to line.

---

[2] *The Abingdon Bible Commentary* (Nashville: Abingdon Press 1929), p. 154.

The Technique of Chanting

As the practice of chanting is confined largely to psalms and a few New Testament hymns, several appropriate instructions should be given.

1. The text must be sung in what approximates the free rhythm of speech. There is no pulse, no beat count on the chanting tone; the words are recited (or intoned) on given pitches.

2. Anglican chant, which replaced Gregorian chant in many Protestant denominations, is "mixed" chant. That is, it uses both chanting tones and measured music such as is found in hymns. The singer must shift rhythmic gears as he uses free rhythm on the chant tones and changes to the normal counting process in the measured sections. This technique may be applied to the first section of the "Jubilate Deo" (Psalms 100), which has traditionally been chanted in the Anglican service.

Notice that no time signature is given. The first notational symbol is not really a whole note but simply a mark indicating the pitch on which the opening words are to be intoned. Having sung (or intoned) "O be joyful in the Lord" in the rhythm of speech, we are suddenly confronted with a measure containing two half notes. This and all other measures will assume a 2/2 time signature, with the half notes sung fairly rapidly. A fast tempo is necessary so that the chant will retain its speechlike quality even though it involves alternating between chanting and measured singing. In the excerpt above, the letters C and M indicate the chanted and measured portions.

Other psalms frequently used in the Anglican tradition are the Venite (Psalms 95), the Bonum Est (Psalms 92), and the De Profundis (Psalms 130).

New Testament Hymns

When Paul mentions "psalms and hymns and spiritual songs," he undoubtedly refers to three distinct forms of worship music—the Old Testament psalms, new hymns of the Christian movement, and spiritual songs or ecstatic improvisations that were never recorded. The following New Testament materials are significant:

1. HYMNS FROM LUKE. Many scholars believe that the hymns recorded in the first two chapters of Luke were contemporary hymns that Luke in his narrative attributed to Mary, Zechariah, the Angelic Choir, and Simeon. Whatever their origin, the Magnificat, the Benedictus, the Gloria in Excelsis, and the Nunc Dimittis are clearly reminiscent of the psalms both in structure and in style. They are the earliest complete Christian hymns extant.

2. HYMN FRAGMENTS. The Pauline and Pastoral Epistles and the Revelation of John contain brief fragments that seem to have been extracted from hymns then in use. Ephesians 5:14 appears to be a portion of an evangelistic hymn; 1 Timothy 3:16 is an early creedal hymn; and 2 Timothy 2:11-13 is a hymn for baptism. Many odes are scattered throughout the Revelation of John. These frag-

ments, unlike the Lukan hymns, contain none of the characteristics of Hebrew poetry but appear to be patterned after Greek literature of the period.

New Testament hymns are filled with praise, gratitude, and hope. They celebrate the Christ event with enthusiasm and joy. That early Christians actually sang these hymns is clear from the record. Pliny the Younger reported to the Emperor Trajan that the worst offense of the Christians was gathering before dawn on an appointed day (Sunday) and singing hymns of praise to Christ as God.

Hymns From the East and West

For centuries the Greek hymns used in connection with worship in Alexandria, Jerusalem, and Byzantium, and the Latin hymns used by the western branch of the church centered in Rome remained untranslated. The ancient hymns and liturgies were first translated into English in connection with the Oxford Movement, an attempt among nineteenth-century Anglicans to reclaim the spirit and assert the authority of the early church. The efforts of John Mason Neale, the "prince of translators," led to the publication of *Translations of Medieval Hymns and Sequences* (1852) and *Hymns of the Eastern Church* (1862), collections of Latin and Greek hymns, respectively.

Early Greek Hymns

* "Shepherd of Eager Youth"—Clement of Alexandria (c. 160-c. 215)
* "Lord Jesus, Think on Me"—Synesius (c. 375-430)
* "Let All Mortal Flesh Keep Silence"—Liturgy of St. James (c. fifth century)

H. Leigh Bennett speaks of Greek hymns as being notable for their "faculty of sustained praise." [3] Although "Shepherd

---
[3] Julian, *op. cit.*, I, 465.

of Eager Youth" was the earliest metrical hymn to be translated, it evidences far more of the translator than of the author. "Lord Jesus, Think on Me" introduces the subjectivity of later hymns in which pure praise was supplanted by concern for human feelings. "Let All Mortal Flesh" is a deeply mystical communion hymn that, when sung to the modal French tune "Picardy," has an aura of ancient, mysterious beauty.

Hymns from Mar Saba

"Christian! Dost Thou See Them?"—Andrew of Crete (660-732)

"Art Thou Weary, Art Thou Troubled?"—Stephen, the Sabaite (c. 725-815)

"The Day of Resurrection" and "Come, Ye Faithful, Raise the Strain"—John of Damascus (c. 676-c. 780)

By the latter part of the second century heretical doctrines began to appear within the Christian movement. In the East Gnosticism exalted general knowledge above knowledge of God. In the West Arianism taught that Christ was an intermediate being between God and the world. Although these heresies ultimately were condemned, this period of theological controversy stimulated the composition of hymns to promote one doctrine or another. At times this promotion took the form of street processions in which antagonists tried to outsing one another. The hymns of the period that dealt with doctrinal controversy are, of course, long since forgotten. The hymns written by the monks of Mar Saba, a monastery outside Jerusalem, were concerned not only with dangers from without but also with the conflict between good and evil within the life of the individual. "Christian! Dost Thou See Them?" and "Art Thou Weary, Art Thou Troubled?" affirm the victory over sin and death that faith in Christ will bring.

Early Latin Hymns

- "We Praise Thee, O God" (Te Deum)—Niceta of Remesiana (c. 335-c. 414)
- "O Splendor of God's Glory Bright"—Ambrose of Milan (340-97)
- "All Glory, Laud, and Honor"—Theodulph of Orleans (c. 760-821)
- "Come, Holy Ghost, Our Souls Inspire"—Rabanus Maurus (?-856)

Ambrose, one of the most important of the church fathers in the West, combatted the Arian heresy by composing orthodox hymns and teaching them to his congregation. His verses consisted of four lines of eight syllables each, a metrical form that later came to be known as "long meter." These hymns, constituting a body of material referred to as "Ambrosian," must have been musically pleasing, for Augustine, after hearing them in Ambrose's church, wrote: "What tears I shed over the hymns and canticles, when the sweet music of thy church thrilled my soul!" [4]

That early Latin hymns were patterned after those produced in the Eastern World is shown by a comparison of Ambrose's "O Splendor of God's Glory Bright" and "Hail, Gladdening Light." The subject matter and use of symbolism are quite similar. And in the noble Te Deum we find that quality of sustained praise found in the Eastern hymns.

Gregory the Great (540?-604), *probably* systematized the church song of his day, doubling the number of modes or scales handed down from the time of Ambrose, collecting the hymns and their melodies, and instituting instruction for the clergy in the system of chanting that bears his name. By the sixth century ~~fear of heresy and~~ the development of a more highly organized ritual caused the virtual abandonment of congregational singing. Although trained priests

---

[4] *Confessions* (IX).

sang most of the service music, the congregation was permitted to participate in the Alleluia that concluded the Gradual—a Psalm chanted between the epistle and the gospel readings. In order to give the deacon time to move from one side of the altar to the other, the Alleluia was extended by adding a series of slurred tones to the final syllable. In the ninth century someone conceived the idea of writing words for these melodies, thus making them easier for the congregation to remember. At first unrhymed and unmetrical, these texts were called proses. When rhyme and meter were adopted, especially through the contribution of Notker Balbulus (840-910), they became known as sequences. So important was this development as a step toward later metrical hymnody that McCutchan says of his contribution: "In form, content, and musical phrasing, Notker's work was entirely original—a practical, musical, and liturgical innovation as great as had been that of Ambrose." [5]

Latin Hymns of the Middle Ages

"Jesus, the Very Thought of Thee"—ascribed to Bernard of Clairvaux (1091-1153)

"All Creatures of Our God and King"—Francis of Assisi (1182-1226)

"O Come, O Come, Immanuel"—Anonymous (twelfth century)

"O Sacred Head, Now Wounded"—Anonymous (fourteenth century)

"Good Christian Men, Rejoice"—Anonymous (fourteenth century)

By the time of the Middle Ages (1000-1400) moral and spiritual decadence infested the church. For the most part, authors of the period accepted these evils as inevitable and

[5] Robert Guy McCutchan, *Hymns in the Lives of Men* (New York and Nashville: Abingdon-Cokesbury Press, 1945), p. 115.

in their hymns lost themselves by contemplating the perfection of Jesus, the glories of heaven, and the horrors of hell! Human feelings now became predominant. In hymns such as "Jesus, the Very Thought of Thee" and "O Sacred Head" the worshiper becomes deeply involved in a mystical experience. The pronouns in these hymns are highly personal. Lines such as

> "Jesus, the very thought of Thee
> With sweetness fills *my* breast"

and

> "Lo, here *I* fall, *my* Saviour!
> 'Tis *I* deserve Thy place"

exemplify the extreme subjectivism of later Latin hymnody.

Hymns of the German Reformation
1. EARLY REFORMATION HYMNS

"A Mighty Fortress Is Our God"—Martin Luther (1483-1546)

"O Morning Star, How Fair and Bright"—Philipp Nicolai (1556-1608)

The German counterpart to the sequences consisted of short metrical hymns in the German language known as *Leichan* that could be sung on festival occasions when the restriction of Latin texts and Gregorian melodies did not apply. The Germans, tremendously fond of the *Leichan*, responded enthusiastically to Luther's call for congregational hymn singing in the language of the people. To provide these hymns, Luther and his friends began to write texts and compose tunes. *Geistliche Kirchengesangbüchlein*, the hymnal of the Reformation, edited jointly by

Luther and Johann Walther, appeared in 1530. "A Mighty Fortress," from the first wave of German hymns, epitomizes through its text and tune the strength and vitality of the Reformation movement. "O Morning Star," at times referred to as the "Queen of Chorales," is the <u>finest hymn of the latter part of the sixteenth century.</u> 157 ⟨5⟩

2. THIRTY YEARS' WAR HYMNS

"Ah, Holy Jesus, How Hast Thou Offended"—Johann Heerman (1585-1647)

"Now Thank We All Our God"—Martin Rinkart (1586-1649)

"If Thou But Suffer God to Guide Thee"—Georg Neumark (1621-81)

During these troubled times unrelieved suffering led to the writing of hymns that expressed deep personal faith in the goodness of God. The brave affirmation of "A Mighty Fortress" is supplanted by the assurance of deliverance by a God who will "free us from all ills in this world and the next." What resources of faith Rinkart must have had that, serving a parish in which because of pestilence and war he had as many as forty funerals a day, he could still write the most "thankful" hymn in our heritage:

> Now thank we all our God
>   With heart and hands and voices,
> Who wondrous things hath done,
>   In whom His world rejoices;
> Who, from our mothers' arms,
>   Hath blessed us on our way
> With countless gifts of love,
>   And still is ours today.

"Ah, Holy Jesus" is an extremely poignant hymn that envisions the author (and presumably every other person) as being guilty of bringing about Jesus' crucifixion. When sung to Crüger's plaintive tune, this is a moving hymn of penitence.

"If Thou But Suffer God to Guide Thee," the text and tune of which were written by Georg Neumark, has much in common with both hymns just mentioned. Its minor tune and its subjective text are not unlike "Ah, Holy Jesus." Yet it contains also the assurance of God's care noted in Rinkart's great hymn; Neumark puts it this way:

> God never yet forsook at need
> The soul who trusted Him indeed.

3. Transitional Hymns

"O Sacred Head, Now Wounded"—Paul Gerhardt (1607-76)

"Come, My Soul, Thou Must Be Waking"—Friedrich von Canitz (1654-99)

Writing in the period following the Thirty Years' War, Gerhardt in "O Sacred Head" forsakes completely the virile style of Luther and Rinkart in favor of the more tender treatment that reached its zenith in the Pietistic period. As Bailey points out, if Luther's God was a fighter and a stickler for dogma, Gerhardt's God was a loving person; and while his hymns followed Reformation doctrines, the creedal concepts were always subordinated to human values.[6]

"Come, My Soul" is a perfect morning hymn, combining gratitude for the new day with the petition that God may prosper every good endeavor and thwart every evil thought and act. In addition to its message the hymn is notable for its effective language, its interesting meter, and its beautiful tune, adapted from a string quartet by the noted composer, Franz Joseph Haydn.

[6] *Op. cit.*, p. 326.

4. Pietistic Hymns

> "Praise to the Lord, the Almighty"—Joachim Neander (1650-80)
>
> "Fairest Lord Jesus"—Anonymous
>
> "Sing Praise to God Who Reigns Above"—Johann J. Schütz (1640-90)

By the late seventeenth century formalism in worship seemed to sap Lutheranism of its earlier vitality. Congregational singing of the chorales was dominated by the choir and organ. Between stanzas skilled organists improvised extended interludes that drew the attention of the congregation away from the text to the performer. The Pietistic movement, initiated in 1650 by Philipp Spener, took the form of cottage prayer meetings and re-emphasized the importance of personal devotion. This movement, a second Reformation, inspired the writing of many hymns, one of the finest of which is "Praise to the Lord," which Dearmer called a "magnificent song of praise, perhaps the finest there is, when we consider the tune." [7] Though not as well-known, "Sing Praise to God" has the same quality of majestic exaltation.

5. Moravian Hymns

> "O Thou to Whose All-searching Sight" and "Jesus, Thy Blood and Righteousness"—Nicolaus von Zinzendorf (1700-60)

The spiritual descendents of John Hus, who first were known as Bohemian Brethren and later as Moravians, arrived in 1722 in Saxony, where they merged with the German Pietists. After the martyr's death of Hus in 1415, his followers continued to defy ecclesiastical restrictions by writing and singing hymns in their own language. As early as 1501, sixteen years before Luther's dramatic entrance on

---

[7] Quoted in Armin Haeussler, *The Story of Our Hymns* (St. Louis: Eden Publishing House, 1952), p. 61.

the scene, the Bohemian Brethren published a hymnal—the first of a "protesting" group. Nicolaus L. Zinzendorf, on whose estate in Herrnhut, Saxony, they took refuge, became their spiritual and organizational leader and later led them in their emigration to the New World. The Moravians are important not only for the significance of their own unusual musical accomplishments both in Europe and America but also for the influence they had on John Wesley and on the hymns of the Wesleyan Revival.

6. Eighteenth- and Nineteenth-Century Hymns

"When Morning Gilds the Skies"—Anonymous

"Silent Night, Holy Night"—Joseph Mohr (1792-1848)

Few great German hymns appeared after 1800. After centuries of religious conflict, relative calm settled over the land. The resulting lethargy together with the rationalism of eighteenth-century theology discouraged the writing of hymns. With such exceptions as are listed above, from 1800 on we must look to England and America for our growing body of hymns.

General Characteristics of German Hymn Tunes

The Reformation chorales represent Christendom's first cohesive body of tunes. When studied in combination with their texts, the chorales are seen to possess the following characteristics:

1. The tunes are stately and dignified, containing few trivial rhythmic patterns. Compare "Ein' feste Burg" ("A Mighty Fortress") with a tune such as "Standing on the Promises."

2. Texts and tunes belong together; tunes are seldom used for other than the original texts. The tunes express the spirit of the texts.

3. German hymns are written in a wide variety of meters. "A Mighty Fortress" (8. 7. 8. 7. 6. 6. 6. 6. 7.) and "Praise to the Lord" (14. 14. 4. 7. 8.) are the only hymns in use employing these meters.

4. All parts—soprano, alto, tenor, and bass—are melodically interesting, due to the superior part writing of J. S. Bach and others. Compare each of the voice parts of "O Sacred Head" with a hymn such as "I Love to Tell the Story."

Metrical Psalms of the Calvinist Movement

During the first century of the German Reformation an opposing movement appeared in Geneva, led by John Calvin. His views regarding congregational song were quite different from those of Luther:

Calvin

Retained no Latin hymns because of their "false doctrine."

Objected to folk tunes because of their frivolous nature.

Claimed that only what God has given in the Bible may be used in worship; hence only settings of Psalms were permitted.

Luther

Retained certain Latin hymns.

Made use of popular folk tunes.

Insisted that man speaks to God in worship; therefore he may compose his own hymns.

Calvin's efforts led to the 1562 publication of the completed French-Genevan Psalter, for which Clément Marot and Théodore de Bèze contributed the metrical versifications and Louis Bourgeois and Claude Guidimel the tunes. The first edition contained unison tunes only, because of

Calvin's opposition to part-singing. One year after Calvin's death, however, Claude Guidimel published a four-part edition.

When Mary became Queen of England in 1553, many English and Scottish Protestants fled to Geneva, where they were exposed to French-Genevan psalms, which they immediately began to translate into English. While in Geneva they published a collection of fifty-one psalms, the Anglo-Genevan Psalter. When Elizabeth became Queen in 1558, Protestantism was restored as the state religion and the refugees returned to England and Scotland, taking their Psalter with them. Even though Queen Bess referred to the metrical psalms as "Geneva jigs," the common people sang them with enthusiasm. The completed "Old Version" of the English Psalter was published in 1562 and is known as the Sternhold and Hopkins version after its two main compilers. This book attempted to provide literal rhymed translations, but some of the verses were so awkward that Samuel Wesley referred to them as "scandalous doggerel." A few of the tunes were borrowed from the French-Genevan Psalter; others were by English composers.

With the Scottish Psalter of 1650 and the Tate and Brady, or "New Version" of the English Psalter of 1696, literalism gave way to paraphrase, making possible a literary grace and poetic quality not found in the "Old Version." Calvin had insisted on tunes so plain and austere that they could not possibly be taken from Latin hymns or the folk songs of the day. In the Tate and Brady version the new-found poetic freedom was accompanied by new melodic and rhythmic interest in the tunes. A comparison of any of the "Old Version" tunes with "Hanover" will dramatize this development.

The following Psalter texts and tunes are found in contemporary hymnals:

Psalters	Texts	Tunes
French-Genevan (1562)		Old 100th, Old 113th, Old 124th, Old 134th
Sternhold and Hopkins (1562)	"All People That on Earth Do Dwell"	St. Flavian Dundee (Windsor) Winchester Old
Scottish (1650)	"The Lord's My Shepherd" "How Lovely Is Thy Dwelling-place"	Dundee (French)
Tate and Brady (1696)	"Through All the Changing Scenes of Life" "As Pants the Hart for Cooling Streams"	St. Anne Hanover

Watts and Wesley—The English Hymn Is Born

The Psalters reigned in England until the logical onslaught of Isaac Watts—philosopher, grammarian, psychologist, theologian, teacher, and hymn writer. Watts is properly known as the "Father of English Hymnody." Although several widely used hymns had already been written, it would have been impossible to compile an English hymnal prior to his contribution. Among the pre-Watts English hymns still in use are: "Let All the World in Every Corner Sing," by George Herbert; "Awake, My Soul, and With the Sun" and "All Praise to Thee, My God, This Night," taken from Thomas Ken's *Manual of Prayers* for Winchester boys. The familiar doxology, "Praise God From Whom All Blessings Flow," was written by Ken as the concluding stanza of each of these hymns.

Charles Wesley, building on Watts's foundation, became the "Sweet Singer of Methodism." Before making a comparative study of England's hymnic giants, it is necessary to recognize the contribution of John Wesley to our story.

While enroute to America, John was tremendously impressed with the witness of a small band of Moravians. In his journal for January 25, 1735, he wrote:

> In the midst of the Psalm wherewith their service began, the sea broke over, split the main sail in pieces . . . A terrible screaming began among the English. The Germans calmly sung on. I asked one of them afterwards, "Was you not afraid?" he answered, "I thank God, No."

Wesley immediately set out to translate Moravian hymns into English, among them Zinzendorf's "O Thou to Whose All-Searching Sight." By 1738 John had returned to London, where on May 24 he had his "heartwarming experience." In the afternoon he was moved by the singing of the De Profundis by the choir of St. Paul's Cathedral. In the evening hymns were sung in connection with the Moravian meeting on Aldersgate Street. God seems to have used sacred song to speak to John Wesley, which may be why he in turn considered hymns so important in spreading the good news of salvation for all. Although most of the hymns of the Wesley Revival were written by Charles, it was John who selected, edited, and arranged them. Henry Bett, in commenting on this unique partnership of the Wesleys, writes:

> It is only when you go through the original volumes of Charles Wesley's verse, and note the way in which his brother chose the best of the hymns, and then omitted from these the weaker

stanzas, until out of a long string of verses of very varied quality there often emerges a hymn of sustained excellence, which is a complete lyric in itself—it is only after such a study that one realizes the excellence of John Wesley's editorial work.[8]

Watts and Wesley Compared

Isaac Watts (1674-1748) *Charles Wesley (1707-1788)*

RELIGIOUS BACKGROUND

Son of a nonconformist parson. | Son of an Anglican priest.

OBJECTIVE IN HYMN WRITING

To Christianize the Psalms, open the way for hymns of human composition, and provide a body of hymns for worship.

To provide hymns that would express the message of the Wesleyan revival and aid in winning souls.

THEIR THEORIES

He maintained that the psalms were not canonical for the New Testament church, for Christ is not mentioned and certain psalms are foreign to New Testament thought.

The Wesleys used hymns to arouse sinners, edify saints, and educate new converts. Their hymnal was a textbook in theology.

SCOPE OF THEIR COMPOSITION

Hymns and Spiritual Songs, 1707. This collection contained free translations of psalms and original hymns based on New Testament texts. *Psalms of David Imi-*

Fifty-six collections of Wesley's hymns were published, culminating in the 1780 hymnal: *A Collection of Hymns for the People Called Methodists.* He wrote 6,500

---

[8] Henry Bett, *The Hymns of Methodism* (3rd ed.; London: The Epworth Press, 1946), p. 10.

tated, 1719. Written in the language of the New Testament, this collection settled the propriety of hymns of human composition.

hymns on every conceivable subject and introduced (*a*) evangelistic hymns and (*b*) hymns of Christian experience.

THEOLOGICAL CONCEPTS

Watts chiefly wrote hymns of praise. As a Calvinist he emphasized the sinfulness of man and the absolute authority of God. As God has foreordained the destiny of every man, there is no call to repentence, only the prayer that the singer may be among the "elect."

Wesley's hymns support the Arminian view that God in his love wills salvation for all. Free grace is proclaimed and sinners are invited to repent. The hymns witness to Christian experience and suggest the possibility of gaining perfection in love through Christ.

LITERARY STYLE

"Watts's hymns are simple in style and language, written down to the level of the common man. Because of the practice of "lining out," he seldom permitted a stop in the middle of a line, and seldom left the end of a line without one. . . ."⁹ His hymns use mainly the three standard meters—short, common, and long.

Wesley was a master of literary style, employing paradox, hyperbole (emphasis by exaggeration), simile, metaphor, and other literary devices. He wrote in many meters, and his vocabulary was inexhaustible. He may have been the most skilled hymn writer of all time.

REPRESENTATIVE HYMNS

"From All That Dwell Below the Skies"

"Christ, the Lord, Is Risen Today"

⁹ Isaac Watts, *Hymns and Spiritual Songs*, Preface.

"Jesus Shall Reign Where'er the Sun"
"Joy to the World, the Lord Is Come"
"O God, Our Help in Ages Past"
"When I Survey the Wondrous Cross"
"A Charge to Keep I Have"
"Hark, the Herald Angels Sing"
"Love Divine, All Loves Excelling"
"O For a Thousand Tongues to Sing"

Additional Eighteenth-Century Hymns

Next to Watts and Wesley, the most prolific eighteenth-century English hymnists were John Newton and William Cowper. Low Church Anglicans made wide use of *Olney Hymns*, their collection to which Newton contributed 281 and Cowper 67 hymns. Its objective, according to Newton, was to promote "the faith and comfort of sincere Christians." The following list contains the best known hymns of Newton and Cowper, as well as of other outstanding writers of the period. The theological orientation of each hymn is given along with the name of its author:

"The Spacious Firmament on High"—Joseph Addison—Rationalist (faith through reason)

"Guide Me, O Thou Great Jehovah"—William Williams—Welsh Revivalist

"The God of Abraham Praise"—Thomas Olivers—Hebrew-Christian

"Rock of Ages"—Augustus Toplady—Calvinist

"All Hail the Power of Jesus' Name"—Edward Perronet—Wesleyan

"Glorious Things of Thee Are Spoken"—John Newton—Calvinist

"God Moves in a Mysterious Way"—William Cowper—Calvinist

English Hymns of the Nineteenth Century

In the eighteenth century English hymn writers generally did not seek literary refinement as an end in itself. They wrote not for the educated but, as Watts said, for those "of ~~vulgar~~ (Common) capacities." By the first decade of the nineteenth century hymn writers became literary craftsmen, making use of vivid figures of speech, colorful symbolism, and other stylistic devices associated with the Romantic Period of English literature. Such words as *fiend, worm, rebel,* and *devil,* found frequently in the hymns of Watts and Wesley and their contemporaries, no longer occurred. Literary sensitivity became an active force.

Most of the outstanding nineteenth-century English hymns came from Anglican authors, representing three groups within the communion—Low Church, High Church, and Broad Church. Low Church hymns showed the influence of the Wesleyan Revival with an emphasis on personal religion and individual piety that was meant to bring about the cure of a sick society. High Church Anglicans, unwilling to accept the findings of science or the intrusion of religion into the arena of social and political life, proclaimed the inerrancy of the Scriptures, apostolic succession, the efficacy of liturgy and the sacraments, and the importance of the Christian Year. It was the Tractarian or Oxford Movement of this group that inspired John Mason Neale and others to translate Greek and Latin hymns as a way of reclaiming some of the lost treasures of the early church. The Tractarian position regarding apostolic succession was so compelling that John Newman, Frederick Faber, and Edward Caswall—three of its devotees—left the Anglican Communion and turned to Roman Catholicism.

Many of England's most thoughtful churchmen identified themselves with the third group, known as Broad Church Anglicans. *Low Churchmen* specialized in personal religious experience. *High Churchmen* emphasized the church and its traditions and prerogatives. *Broad Churchmen* acknowledged the merits of both but added a wholesome concern for all life and a responsibility for making the kingdom of God a reality among men.

Scottish Presbyterians, English Congregationalists, and Unitarians also made modest contributions to nineteenth-century English hymnody. However, it is safe to say that if the eighteenth century belonged to Non-Conformist Isaac Watts and to Methodist Charles Wesley (of course, at that time Methodism was a movement within the Anglican church), nineteenth-century England found the Anglican hymn writers and composers front stage and center.

Nineteenth-Century Hymn Tunes

In the nineteenth century, the prolific writing of hymn texts was accompanied by a deliberate effort on the part of a group of highly trained Anglican composers to provide suitable tunes for the new texts. A factor in this increased productivity of tunes was the first serious effort (in England and America) to assign a tune to each hymn. Previously texts and tunes appeared in separate books, and one tune might be used with several texts. These Anglican composers, among them John B. Dykes, John Stainer, Arthur Sullivan, and Joseph Barnby, commonly known as the "Cathedral School," continue to be widely represented in our hymn books, though their tunes are not now as highly regarded as they once were. The relationship between English Victorian texts and tunes is not nearly as secure as that of German chorales. One would have difficulty, however, in substituting another tune for "Holy, Holy, Holy" or for "Onward, Christian Soldiers."

The most important hymn collection of the century was *Hymns Ancient and Modern*. Statistics substantiate the claim that this was one of the most successful hymnals of all time. Its contribution to later denominational hymnals was enormous. More than a hundred hymn texts and many tunes that now belong to the ecumenical church first saw the light of day in this collection.

Nineteenth-century English hymnody may be characterized as follows:

1. Hymns bore the imprint of the Romantic Movement with colorful language and vivid figures of speech:
    "Holy, Holy, Holy"—Reginald Heber
    "Brightest and Best of the Sons of the Morning"—Reginald Heber

2. Subject matter was taken from nature:
    "For the Beauty of the Earth"—Folliott S. Pierpont
    "God Who Madest Earth and Heaven"—Reginald Heber

3. Low Church hymns were evangelical and personal:
    "Spirit of God, Descend Upon My Heart"—George Croly
    "Take My Life, and Let It Be Consecrated"—Frances R. Havergal

4. Women hymn writers made notable contributions, namely:
    C. Frances Alexander, Frances R. Havergal, and Sarah F. Adams

5. Noted poets turned to hymn writing:
    "Strong Son of God, Immortal Love"—Alfred Tennyson
    "God of Our Fathers, Known of Old"—Rudyard Kipling

6. The Tractarian Movement led to translations from Greek and Latin sources:
    "Jesus, the Very Thought of Thee"—Edward Caswall
    "Christian, Dost Thou See Them?"—John Mason Neale

7. High Church hymns were written by men who espoused Roman Catholicism:
  "Faith of Our Fathers"—Frederick Faber
  "Lead, Kindly Light"—John Henry Newman

8. Broad Church hymns expressed social concern and international responsibility:
  "These Things Shall Be: a Loftier Race"—John Addington Symonds
  "In Christ There Is No East or West"—John Oxenham

9. Tunes were composed to fit specific texts:
  "Onward, Christian Soldiers"—Arthur S. Sullivan
  "I Heard the Voice of Jesus Say"—John B. Dykes

Twentieth-Century English Hymns

To support the claim that creative endeavor persists in the twentieth century in the land of Watts and Wesley, two texts and one tune should be mentioned.

The texts stand in the Broad Church tradition of Tennyson and Kipling, expressing prophetic concern for international integrity and human brotherhood. They are:

  "O God of Earth and Altar"
    —Gilbert K. Chesterton (1906)

  "Turn Back, O Man, Forswear Thy Foolish Ways"
    —Clifford Bax (1919)

The tune—"Sine Nomine"—may well be the finest hymn tune by the greatest English composer of the century. Ralph Vaughan Williams wrote this splendid unison setting for How's "For All the Saints Who From Their Labors Rest."

American Hymnody

The first book to be published on American soil was the 1640 *Bay Psalm Book,* and the first book to be printed on Franklin's printing press was an edition of Watts' hymns. Yet only one hymn of permanent value was actually written on American soil prior to 1800: Timothy Dwight's "I Love Thy Kingdom, Lord." The reason for this apparent paradox is that for the most part the colonists sang psalms and hymns brought over from Europe. While the *Bay Psalm Book* was of American origin, its use was inconsequential compared to that of the English psalters and the hymn collections of Watts and the Wesleys.

Our forefathers had access only to the texts of Watts' and Wesley's hymns; the hymnals of their day did not contain tunes. To find tunes to which these hymns could be sung in America they turned to the folk songs of their heritage. One example is "Foundation," the early American tune used with "How Firm a Foundation." Note its five-tone scale and the regularity of its "dot and dash" rhythm.[10] Other well-known anonymous American folk hymn tunes are "Amazing Grace," "Cleansing Fountain," and "Campmeeting." In spite of their lack of formal musical training, our forefathers in the eighteenth century were more productive of tunes than of texts.

Nineteenth-Century American Hymnody

The substitution of Watts and Wesley for metrical psalmody took place during the first two decades of the century; Timothy Dwight's revision of Watts' *Psalms and Hymns* appeared in 1801. In 1824 *Village Hymns for Social Worship*, by Asahel Nettleton, was published. Designed to be a supplement to Watts' *Psalms and Hymns*, this book was the finest evangelical hymnal yet published in America. *Zion's Harp*, its companion, was the first tune book arranged for a specific collection of texts. Of course, the singer (or at least the leader—often called "precentor") had to manipulate two books, one for the text and one for the tune.

[10] This melody can be played on the black keys of the piano, signifying its pentatonic character.

For many persons *Village Hymns* set too high a standard, and Joshua Leavitt boasted that his collection, *The Christian Lyre* (1831), was not intended to please "scientific musicians." Paradoxically Alexander's translation of Gerhardt's beautiful Passion hymn "O Sacred Head, Now Wounded" first appeared in Leavitt's generally inferior collection. A technical step forward in this book was the printing of a tune for each hymn on the page immediately opposite the text.

Collections like *Village Hymns* and *The Christian Lyre* illustrate the wide disparity of musical tastes that marked this period. To this scene of musical ferment came the giant of church music reform in eighteenth-century America, Lowell Mason (1792-1872).

It was undoubtedly Leavitt's collection to which Mason and his collaborator, Thomas Hastings, referred in the preface of their 1832 collection, *Spiritual Songs for Social Worship*. They mention "the vulgar melodies of the street, of the midnight reveller, of the circus and the ballroom . . . which . . . we are told, are the best adapted to call forth pure and holy emotions, in special seasons of revival." The tunes in *Spiritual Songs,* written mostly by Lowell Mason, were simple and singable, yet dignified. After more than a century Mason remains one of the composers most widely represented in denominational hymnals. The following are a few of the many beloved hymns for which he composed or arranged tunes: "My Faith Looks Up to Thee" ("Olivet"), "When I Survey the Wondrous Cross" ("Hamburg"), "Nearer, My God, to Thee" ("Bethany"), "O for a Thousand Tongues to Sing" ("Azmon"), and "Safely Through Another Week" ("Sabbath").

One more collection must be mentioned, *The Plymouth Collection,* the publication of which was instigated by Henry Ward Beecher in 1851 shortly after he became pastor of the newly organized Plymouth Church in Brooklyn. Arriving there, he found no music in the hands of the congregation; the singing was carried entirely by the paid choir. In the *Plymouth Collection,* for the first time in a major American hymnal, the tune was printed immediately above the words.

As we have seen, during the first half of the nineteenth century many new tunes were composed and ways were developed whereby they could be printed in conjunction with the texts. Relatively few hymn texts were written during the opening decades of the century. Of the sixty American hymns detailed by Bailey, only seven were written prior to 1835.[11]

For the purpose of this study we shall classify American hymns in five categories: (*a*) Evangelical hymns, (*b*) Unitarian hymns, (*c*) "unintentional" hymns of John Greenleaf Whittier, (*d*) gospel songs, and (*e*) hymns expressing social concern and relating religious experience to the whole of life.

Evangelical Hymns

For a succinct definition of the emphasis that produced evangelical hymns, it would be difficult to improve on Bailey's explanation:

> It consisted in cultivating the mystic, personal side: communion with God, fervent love of Christ as God, prayer, contemplation of heaven as the reward for the faithful endurance of the ills of life, nature as an approach to God, the winning of souls through conversion rather than through baptism, the spread of the gospel to all lands.[12]

[11] *Op. cit.,* p. 477.
[12] *Ibid,* p. 482.

OUR HERITAGE OF HYMNS 153

Widely used and greatly loved hymns in this group are:

"My Faith Looks up to Thee"—Ray Palmer—highly Calvinistic with implications of need for sacrificial atonement

"What a Friend We Have in Jesus"—Joseph Scriven—affirms personal faith in Jesus

"More Love to Thee, O Christ"—Elizabeth Prentiss—deals with feelings

"I Need Thee Every Hour"—Annie Hawks—mystical, contemplation

"Still, Still With Thee"—Harriet Stowe—a hymn of God-awareness

"Break Thou the Bread of Life"—Mary Lathbury—a hymn on the "Word," referring to Scripture

Unitarian Hymns

The definitive Unitarian collection, published in 1864 by Samuel Longfellow (brother of Henry Wadsworth Longfellow) and Samuel Johnson, was entitled *Hymns of the Spirit*. Although the authors did not mention Christ in their hymns, the ethical concepts contained were surely those of the Master. Although these New England authors objected to the intellectual irresponsibility of much of traditional doctrine, they did not neglect the need for redeeming men and society through a more vital knowledge of and commitment to God's will as revealed by prophets and teachers throughout the ages. Characteristic Unitarian hymns are:

"Holy Spirit, Truth Divine"—Samuel Longfellow—but with the One God

"Life of Ages, Richly Poured"—Samuel Johnson—God's love revealed in "prophet's word," "thinker's creed," "hero's blood"

"Lord of All Being, Throned Afar"—Oliver Wendell Holmes—most subjective of these hymns: God is "throned afar," "yet to each loving heart, how near!"

These three typical hymns are characterized by (a) absence of references to Christ, (b) highly developed intellectual concepts, and (c) literary excellence.

Hymns of John Greenleaf Whittier (1807-1892)

The "Good, Grey Quaker Poet" has been called an unintentional hymn writer, for his hymns are really selected verses from lyric poems. As we have noted earlier, Whittier's hymns are unexcelled as models of literary excellence. His use of figurative language and the richness of his vocabulary are constantly revealed. But beyond being a skilled craftsman of word and phrase, Whittier wrote as an enlightened, mature Christian. Bailey says of him: "He is greatest because of the depth of his religious insights, the transparent sincerity of their expression and the absence of those divisive views that have in others obscured the underlying unity of our faith. All hymnals could contain Whittier—Unitarian to High Church." [13] Four of his finest hymns, found in most Protestant hymnals, are:

"O Brother Man, Fold to Thy Heart Thy Brother"—from "Worship," a fifteen-stanza poem (See page 51.)

"Dear Lord and Father of Mankind"—from "The Brewing of Soma," a seventeen-stanza poem

"Immortal Love, Forever Full"—from "Our Master," a thirty-eight-stanza poem

"I Know Not What the Future Hath"—from "The Eternal Goodness," a twenty-two-stanza poem

[13] *Op cit.*, p. 534.

Gospel Songs

Although a popular hymnody had been developing throughout the century, the full flowering of the gospel-song movement awaited the arrival of Dwight L. Moody and his song-leading genius, Ira D. Sankey, who in 1871 joined forces and, according to one writer, "reduced the population of hell by a million souls." Many texts of gospel songs were written by a wide assortment of pious but unlettered authors. Outstanding among these was Fanny J. Crosby, a remarkable lady who, in her blindness, found a peace and joy that motivated her to write eight thousand songs. A comparison of any one of her songs with the hymns of Whittier will instantly reveal their differences. Whittier's hymns evidence relevant responsibility to life; Fanny Crosby's are primarily concerned with personal peace and joy.

The tunes of gospel songs provide the main reason for their popularity. Significantly no highly skilled composers contributed to this body of material. Moreover, it is apparent that the tunes were not intended to capture and support the meaning and mood of the texts. (A great hymn is the result of a tune that enhances the text in many ways). The purpose of many gospel song texts was simply to carry a popular and appealing tune.

Hymns of Personal Responsibility and Social Concern

The contents of this chapter have revealed varied and sometimes opposing forces at work. Stern Calvinistic theology elicited an antidote in the form of liberal Unitarianism, and each of these movements provided hymns of merit. Because neither type spoke to the nineteenth-century revivalists, gospel songs came to be written, widely sung, and greatly loved. Between the extremes of these cross-currents, we found John Greenleaf Whittier, who retained the Christ-centered devotional warmth of the Evangelicals while accepting the intellectual disciplines of the Liberals. In a real sense Whittier was the first of a number of American hymnists who followed in the train of the Broad Church group in England. To these men religious experience was not *apart* from life but *a part* of life. What the mind cannot accept as true, the emotions cannot accept as valid. Moreover, what the mind accepts as true and right, the individual and society must accept as binding to both personal and group behavior. The hymns contributed by these writers imply that religion is the central fact in life, affecting every situation faced and every decision reached. One cannot sing these hymns thoughtfully and act the rogue. Their content reminds us that Sunday worship and Monday business are both a part of the whole cloth of living. The best of them recognize the omnipotence of God, the lordship of Christ, and the responsibility of Christian discipleship. Accordingly they deal with personal and social responsibility, with peace and brotherhood, with bringing Jesus' teachings into the arena of everyday life. The following are among the finest American hymns of personal responsibility and social concern:

"Once to Every Man and Nation"—James Russell Lowell—excerpt from "The Present Crisis," a protest against slavery

"O Master, Let Me Walk With Thee"—Washington Gladden—a prayer not to be freed from trouble but strengthened for service

"This Is My Father's World"—Maltbie D. Babcock—an interpretation of God, man, and the world that God has made

"Where Cross the Crowded Ways of Life"—Frank M. North—the earliest hymn on social concern and home missions

"Joyful, Joyful, We Adore Thee"—Henry van Dyke—recognizes God's goodness and inspires us to live as brothers

"Rise Up, O Men of God"—William P. Merrill—a straightforward, urgent call to discipleship

"God of Grace and God of Glory"—Harry Emerson Fosdick—a prayer for power to cooperate with God in bringing in the kingdom

Hymnody Today

As we deepen our own knowledge and appreciation of the hymns of our heritage, we cannot help feeling grateful to the inspired, consecrated authors and composers whose labors made possible this heritage. We are grateful also to those who have altered, arranged, and edited, to the enrichment of our hymnody. With the riches of this heritage available, hymnals now being developed should be the finest ever given to the Christian community. In each generation excellent new hymns are written, and, as a result of rising standards, less worthy hymns are gradually excised. Increased sensitivity on the part of hymnal revision committees results in more careful mating of texts and tunes. Good texts, formerly set to inferior tunes, are being combined with tunes that are more worthy of them. Hymns are now placed in more singable keys. In these and other ways denominational hymnals constantly are being improved in order to provide the finest possible body of hymns for use in Christian worship.

In this study we have insisted that more than a superior body of hymns is required. The hymns must be *understood*, *loved*, and *sung* by the people—children, youth, and adults. There are specific ways in which this ideal is being more generally approximated than ever before:

1. The parish minister is more knowledgeable in hym-

nody, having had courses in church music and hymnody at the seminary level.

2. Churches are engaging part-time and full-time directors of music who have a working knowledge of hymn use and appreciation.

3. Church schools, guided by directors of Christian education and competent lay teachers, are placing more emphasis on careful selection and use of hymns.

4. Churches are developing graded choir programs in which persons of all ages are guided in serious hymn study.

With these developments across the church, there is reason to believe that we have reached the time when hymn singing, approached more seriously and conscientiously than ever before, will begin to achieve God's purpose for it.

> "Make a joyful noise unto the Lord, all ye lands,
> Serve the LORD with gladness: come before his presence with singing! [14]

---

[14] Psalms 100:1-2 (KJV).

BIBLIOGRAPHY

Books

Bailey, Albert E. *The Gospel in Hymns.* New York: Charles Scribner's Sons, 1950.

Benson, Louis F. *The Hymnody of the Christian Church.* Richmond: John Knox Press, 1956.

Bett, Henry. *The Hymns of Methodism.* 3rd ed. London: The Epworth Press, 1946.

Davis, Arthur Paul. *Isaac Watts, His Life and Works.* New York: The Dryden Press, 1943.

Flew, R. N. *The Hymns of Charles Wesley.* London: The Epworth Press, 1953.

Foote, Henry Wilder. *Three Centuries of American Hymnody.* Cambridge: Harvard University Press, 1940; Hamden, Conn.: Shoe String Press, 1961.

Frost, M. *English and Scottish Psalm and Hymn Tunes, 1543-1677.* London: Oxford University Press, 1953.

Haeussler, Armin. *The Story of Our Hymns.* St. Louis: Eden Publishing House, 1952.

Ingram, Madeline D. *Organizing and Directing Children's Choirs.* Nashville: Abingdon Press, 1959.

Julian, John J. *A Dictionary of Hymnology.* 2nd revised ed. 2 vols. New York: Dover Publications, Inc., 1907.

Lovelace, Austin C. *An Anatomy of Hymnody.* Nashville: Abingdon Press, 1965.

———. *The Organist and Hymn Playing,* Nashville: Abingdon Press, 1962.

Lovelace, Austin C., and William C. Rice. *Music and Worship in the Church.* Nashville: Abingdon Press, 1960.

McCutchan, Robert Guy. *Hymn Tune Names: Their Sources and Significance.* Nashville: Abingdon Press, 1957.

———. *Our Hymnody: A Manual of the Methodist Hymnal.* Nashville: Abingdon Press, 1937.

Manning, Bernard L. *The Hymns of Wesley and Watts.* London: The Epworth Press, 1942.

Mathis, William S. *The Pianist and Church Music.* Nashville: Abingdon Press, 1962.

Messenger, Ruth Ellis. *The Medieval Latin Hymn.* Washington: Capital Press, 1953.

Morsch, Vivian Sharp. *The Use of Music in Christian Education.* Philadelphia: The Westminster Press, 1956.

Rattenbury, J. Ernest. *The Evangelical Doctrines of Charles Wesley's Hymns.* 3rd ed. Naperville, Ill.: Alec R. Allenson, Inc. 1954; London: The Epworth Press, 1941, 1954.

———. *The Eucharistic Hymns of John and Charles Wesley.* Naperville, Ill.: Alec R. Allenson, Inc., 1948; London: The Epworth Press, 1948.

Routley, Erik. *The English Carol.* New York: Oxford University Press, 1958; London: Jenkins, Ltd., 1958.

———. *Hymns Today and Tomorrow.* Nashville: Abingdon Press, 1964.

———. *I'll Praise My Maker.* London: Independent Press, 1951.

———. *The Music of Christian Hymnody.* Naperville, Ill.: Alec R. Allenson, Inc., 1957; London: Independent Press, 1957.

Sydnor, James R. *The Hymn and Congregational Singing.* Richmond: John Knox Press, 1960.

Thomas, Edith Lovell. *Music in Christian Education.* Nashville: Abingdon Press, 1953.

Recordings

Great Hymns for Children. "Heritage in Hymnody" series. Albums 1-6. 33 1/3 rpm, 12 inch. Nashville: Graded Press.

Hymn of the Month: Twelve Hymns for the Christian Year. Album 1. 33 1/3 rpm, 12 inch. Nashville: Graded Press, 1963-64.

Hymn of the Month: Twelve Hymns for the Christian Year. Album 2. 33 1/3 rpm, 12 inch. Nashville: Graded Press, 1964-65.

Music for Worship: Two records of Hymns, Anthems, and Organ Music. 33 1/3 rpm, 12 inch. Nashville: Graded Press.